John Pimlott

The Trout Fisherman's Bedside Book

by Arthur R. Macdougall, Jr.

ILLUSTRATED BY JOHN PIMLOTT

SIMON AND SCHUSTER

NEW YORK

1963

FIRST PRINTING

Library of Congress Catalog Card Number: 63–14564
Manufactured in the United States of America
Printed by The Murray Printing Co., Forge Village, Mass.
Bound by The Book Press, Brattleboro, Vermont

To My Grandsons
Arthur Raymond Dingley
and
Arthur Cameron Macdougall

Contents

8 *Contents*

THE ANTIQUITY OF ANGLING

Then, first, for the antiquity of angling, of which I shall not say much, but only this: some say it is as ancient as Deucalion's flood; others, that Belus, who was the first inventor of godly and virtuous recreations, was the first inventor of angling; and some others say, for former times have had their disquisitions about the antiquity of it, that Seth, one of the sons of Adam, taught it to his sons, and that by them it was derived to posterity; others say that he left it engraven on those pillars which he erected, and trusted to preserve the knowledge of mathematics, music, and the rest of that precious knowledge, and those useful arts which, by God's appointment or allowance, and his noble industry, were thereby preserved from perishing in Noah's flood.

The Compleat Angler

John Pimlott

Adam Was the Father

of All Anglers

I READ in the first book of the Bible, "And a river ran out of Eden to water the garden." Why should one doubt that there were fish in that river? And since the place was Eden, the fish in that river were *trout*. I do not mean any old trout, such as European brown trout. I mean *Salvelinus fontinalis*.

But if one must accept such aspects of the truth as are known as "sober facts," he might admit that the trout in Eden were smallish trout, since the beginning had only begun, and it is a "sober fact" that trout grow slowly. However, it is probable that "sober facts" had not been invented. Look at that serpent that could speak Hebrew or whatever tongue it was that Eve understood. Does a talking snake, and so eloquent a snake, sound like a "sober fact"? Certainly not. Indeed, why should we believe that Yahweh created the "sober fact"? And therefore it is feasible to presume that the trout in the river that ran out of Eden were lusty, lustrous, and larger.

Furthermore, the river that watered the garden

must have been inhabited by every creeping thing, such as nymphs of the alder fly, the fish fly, the dobson fly, the May fly, the eel fly, the damsel fly, the darning and damning fly, the stone fly, the tenspot, and so on, world without end.

Only an old-time angler could imagine the hush and beauty of that first hatch on that river where the world was new. We may suppose the *Ephemeridea* appeared in such winged multitudes that the whisper of their fragile wings was heard in the land of Havilah.[1] And then began the first rise of trout. *Salvelinus fontinalis* rose up in all his glory and fed on that hatch for forty days and forty nights. So he grew prodigiously. And Adam saw that it was good.

Adam went fishing for trout. One need not be reminded that the traditional version tells us that Adam ate some fruit. And that fruit had grown on the tree of life, the tree of the knowledge of good and evil. Later, Adam acted thickheaded for a man who had eaten anything like that. In fact, he acted as dull as a bad boy who had just smoked his first cigar. But men have always agreed that whatever sin Adam did sin, we did all sin in Adam. I am not challenging that in this place, although I suspect that Adamology. Aside from that, it seems to me that no one knows what Adam ate, because the Book does not say. He only ate of the fruit that had been forbidden.

But Adam went fishing for trout. And he came home after a long day on the river. He found that Eve had changed. She was cool. The serpent had been talking to her. And that serpent was the most cunning

[1] Do not ask me where is Havilah. I fear it is only a sober fact these days, although it was once a land of gold and precious gems.

of all creeping things. In short, he had been insinuating. And for a beginner in the beginning he was astonishingly skillful in the use of insinuation.[2] He said, "Have you considered, my dear Eve, that no one knows what Adam is doing when he claims to be fishing for trout?" Eve considered that. And she said to the serpent, "Let's not be silly. Since I am the only woman in the world, I need not worry." Then the serpent smiled a serpentile smile and asked, "How do you know?" So Eve had been brooding over that serpent's remark. And when Adam came, she began to berate him.

Dear old Adam tried to hush her with a glowing tale of the big one that got away. Eve became more and more furious and threatened to return his rib and leave him flat. At that, Adam heard a low, hissy snicker; and he beheld the glint of evil in the snake's eyes. Here was something to let go on. Leaping to action, he hurled a stone hatchet at the serpent, which insinuated itself under the doorstep with the door mat that said WELCOME on it. Adam read what the mat said and began to shout, waving his arms and stamping about. He went so far in his fury as to kick the cat, which was only a kitten in those days.

Thus began and ended the first family row. Our innocent but stupid ancestors were disgraced. Elohim[3] drove them out of Eden. Heavy of heart, and full of sorrow, Adam took his rod, gear, and a bottle of citronella, and went off down the river, leaving Eve to raise Cain.

---

[2] When the word "insinuation" is pronounced as it should be, one hears it crawl like a serpent.

[3] That is the name Genesis uses in the Hebrew for God or gods.

Be assured that there is no moral to this, none whatsoever. The book of Genesis makes it plain that Adam and Eve were created before morals were invented. Anyhow, Adam fished out his sulk and sorrow and came back home, where he apologized to Elohim and Eve. But he continued to fish for trout, and to beget fishermen, which accounts for you and me.

BUT ANGLING IS AN ART

O sir, doubt not but that angling is an art; is it not an art to deceive a trout with an artificial fly? a trout, that is more sharp-sighted than any hawk you have named, and more watchful and timorous than your high-mettled merlin is bold? And yet, I doubt not to catch a brace or two to-morrow, for a friend's breakfast. Doubt not therefore, sir, but that angling is an art, and an art worth your learning.

Piscator, in The Compleat Angler

that I told you, here in this room where it is dry, warm, and cozy, that one seldom gets hold of a trout, or a rainbow, or a salmon, when the river is running high and white. They do not feed under such conditions. Would you attempt to eat during an earthquake or with a raging flood pouring into your house?" It was a long speech. The doctor did not hear it.

I did venture to inquire, as we left the house, if he was properly equipped. He said he was. Therefore I did not take any flies or my rod. I did take my landing net, which was a silly gesture, and I knew it.

The big west gate in the dam, high up on the ledge, was open, and a crazy white river surged across the big pool to the shore on the other side. The situation was hopeless for fishing. Then! As if to cap the climax, or mock the crisis, the doctor pulled out a nicely stocked dry-fly book—dry flies for that wild pool of plunging water! I waved my net at him, as a Roman lady in Nero's time might have waved her lily hand at a dying gladiator. And I yelled at him above the roar of the river, "Go ahead. Fish your fool head off." And he went ahead. He tried for thirty minutes to fish with a dry fly in all that mad discharge of river water. And if there is anything more like the utterness of nothing than a dry fly in such white water, I have not seen it, or even heard about it.

After that, the doctor looked at me. And what was it that the doctor wanted to say? Did he admit that a dry fly was useless, indeed helpless, in water like that? No. The doctor said, "I don't believe that there is a fish in this place. I even doubt that there has been a fish in this place." As men say up this way, when they mean something, "That didn't set well with me." The implication seemed to be that if there were fish in the river, he, the doctor, would have raised those fish, rain or no rain, whatever or whatever. But I still endeavored to look like a good Samaritan. I pointed to a narrow slick of water about four feet wide, near the shore. It was the only place where a trout might rest and where a dry fly might float a few seconds. Why the doctor had disdained to fish it, I do not know.

Then I yelled in his ear. "Are you sure that there isn't some sort of a *wet* fly in that book of yours?"

"I never fish wet," he said. But he began to search. And he did find one small moth-eaten Gray Ghost. And he was ashamed. He said, "A fellow who was a total stranger to me insisted that I try this thing last summer when I fished the Madison."

"Try it now," I suggested.

He shrugged his rugged shoulders. "I will tie it on for you, but you are to do the fishing."

I refused to touch the rod. The trickery of it. Trying to show me up. I said to him, "If I had wanted to waste time fishing tonight, I would have brought my own rod and some wet flies. And may I gently remind you that I told you, before we left my house two hours ago, that the river was far too high for fishing?"

Of course this doctor was a gentleman. "All right," he said, smiling at me and my rancor, "I'll try a few casts with the thing, just to show you that a wet fly is as useless as a dry when, as you said, the trout won't rise anyway."

Just to show me, he cast beyond the slick, back into the boiling water. And he went on casting for about ten minutes. The streamer tossed about like a chip. Perhaps that irked the doctor, for he turned on me with something like a trace of temper in his voice and a bit of it in his manner. "You claim that there are

trout, salmon, and rainbow in this river. You have
written about fishing in this river and catching fish in
this river. Show me!" He thrust his rod into my right
hand. If I had not grasped it, it would have gone into
the river. Anyhow, to have done that was a natural
reaction. But I did not propose to accept the challenge.
I had been at pains to make him understand.

The doctor saw the look in my eyes. He guessed my
thought. "Go ahead," he urged. "Just try it. We both
understand that conditions are the worst and the fish
few and far between, if any."

I looked at the gray, angry river. I looked at the
stiff little rod. I looked at the old Gray Ghost. Poor old
Gray Ghost. Doubtless fly makers could tie a better
streamer fly, but doubtless none of them have.[1] I decided to give it a chance. The very feel of a good rod
in one's hand is an invitation to use it. I cast the fly
into the slick. I cast it once, and a handsome trout
cleared the water. The trout meant business, but I
managed to jerk the fly away from him. And I said to
the doctor, "Did you see that trout?" He admitted
that he had seen it. I shoved the butt of the rod at him
and said, "Then get him."

He protested like a gentleman that the trout was
my fish, but I did not yield to him. He cast where we
had seen the trout rise, and the trout slashed at the
fly and hooked itself. After a few moments of being
washed about in that choking white water, the trout
led in to us. And I never netted a trout with more
satisfaction. He weighed two pounds. A handsome fellow. And the doctor began to fish again. But after two
minutes or so of fishing the slick, he became discour-

[1] Yes, I remember what Izaak Walton said about the strawberry.

aged and went back to longer casts into the pool. After a while of that he thrust his rod at me again. And he said, with a smile, "You did it once. Let's see you do it again."

I had done it once, and that was reason enough for refusing to try again. Let good enough be good enough, and the extraordinary go unchallenged. On the other hand, did the man doubt that I could do it again?

The appearance of the little Gray Ghost had not improved. It looked sadder than ever, bereft and all that. I cast down into the slick. The rainy night was near at hand. The night was a blackness on the mountains to the west of the river. It was a dismal presence over the pool. I wished that we had gone home when the doctor caught the trout. I cast six times. The pool began to look like the ancient void in which there were no trout, no fish of any kind. I cast one more cast. And a salmon rose like a shadow. I pulled the fly from under his wide mouth, and I said to the doctor in the rain, "Did you see that?"

"I certainly did." And that time he needed no urging to take his rod. He cast. The salmon struck. The doctor worked hard, but it was twenty minutes before he had that fish in a mood to be netted. It only weighed three pounds. The trout and the salmon were not *big* fish, but they were a great satisfaction to me.

We drove back to my house. The doctor's wife was waiting for him, whether patiently or impatiently I cannot say. But she said, "Did you get some fish?" I went to the refrigerator to store his trout and his salmon, but I heard his answer. "Yes, I caught two beautiful fish, a trout and a salmon. However, but for this fellow, Macdougall, I could not have found a fish. In fact I didn't find a fish. This fellow is a wizard."

Thus endeth the lesson. He who has ears to hear, let him hear. It is in that way that reputations, dreadful and fearful to sustain, are made.[2] I should have gone back from the kitchen to explain to the lady and to her doctor that my casts into the slick had been wildly and incredibly lucky. Alas, I did not tell them. So the doctor and his wife went home, far from where flows the Kennebec, and they may still think that I am a wizard, particularly when fishing with an old Gray Ghost streamer fly.

[2] Like going over Niagara in a barrel. Do it once, and the crowd will insist you must do it again.

AND NOW FOR THE ART OF CATCHING FISH

Now for the art of catching fish, that is to say, how to make a man that was none, to be an angler by a book. He that undertakes it shall undertake a harder task than Mr. Hales (a most valiant and excellent fencer) who, in a printed book called A Private School of Defence, *undertook to teach that art or science, and was laughed at for his labour . . . because that art was not to be taught by words, but practice; and so must angling.*

Introduction, The Compleat Angler

The Old-Fashioned Rules

MAYBE THIS IS the first commandment for trouters: Go gently, go easily, and relax and relax. And this is the way one began to do it. First, he cut a pole. That pole was often an alder, because when one bent an alder near its butt, it was easily and quickly cut off. And one could cut it with a jackknife he had purchased at a five-and-ten-cent store for ten cents. When one had cut his pole, he attached the line at the tip end and wound it around and around. When he was ready to fish, he unwound what was needed. No one ever invented a simpler or more satisfactory equipment for small brooks and streams.[1] As for hooks, they were usually about number eights, and a boy purchased them for a cent apiece, or two for a cent, if the man who sold them to you happened to be sympathetic.

Then one dug him a can of worms. The worms were free. But in haying time crickets and grasshoppers were proper bait. Anyhow, once one had assembled this equipment, he fished. What do these anxious technicians mean by how to do it? One might be clumsy when he began, but he learned. Of course there were many "rules," and some of them did not amount to much.

It was a rule to keep quiet. It was against that rule to talk out loud, even to oneself. We were sure the fish could hear us. Another rule was to walk on the side of

[1] What folks meant when they said "brook" and what they meant when they said "stream" has always interested me. In the old parlance, a brook was a small, independent flow of clean water and was spring-fed. On the other hand, a stream is smaller than a river, as a brook is smaller than a stream, although in some places a brook is called a stream and a stream is a river, because there are no rivers.

the brook where one's shadow fell off on the bank and
not into the brook. And we *eased* the baited hook
down the current, or we *eased* it into a pool. Splashes
were outlawed. And if anyone had suggested that we
might wade up the brook or down the brook, we
should have deemed him insane. To be *careful* was
the fundamental rule. Boys who were not careful
about anything else took no ends of pains when they
were fishing for trout. Why not? If one dropped a
stone into a pool, or just splashed water, he saw the
frightened trout darting about. *Careful* was the rule.

And one always kept his hook covered up, some
anyway. Sum it up this way: Don't make a noise.
Fish slowly. Do some waiting now and then. Keep
oneself out of sight. Keep one's shadow off the water.
That was about all there was to it, Mister. That was
how to do it. And after all these years, I believe that is
about all there is to trout fishing in a brook, although
I have learned that flies, wet and dry, are handier
than worms, unless the brook is so landscaped with
alders and various bushes that one cannot fish it with
a fly rod.

There is evidence that supports much of the boyhood lore. When the canary at our house is permitted
to fly about the room and comes to rest on the side rail
of the aquarium, the goldfish go to the bottom and
stay there until the finch has flown off. A goldfish is
not as smart as a trout.

And the old tactics were soundly planned. If you
fall into the brook, fall in quietly. And learn to wait.
Keep out of sight. A fisher for trout need not know so
much as the trout, but he certainly needs to know as
much about catching trout as a country boy. And this

is the gist of it all, as it is the reason why brook fishing is an important recreation and discipline: they also catch trout who only stand and wait.[2]

Now it might seem that I failed to appreciate the technician. If that is a sin, I am guilty. I was once invited to go fishing with a man who was inclined to be technical, although he did not fish with flies. He was, so he informed me, an expert wormer. After I had tried to fly-fish on his brook, I understood why he fished with worms. Alders are for keeping brook water cool. Therefore they are for benevolent shade on a brook's right hand and left hand, but alders are a pest to the fly fisherman, roll casts included.

I watched the expert wormer prepare his gear. It was as numerous as a fly-fisherman's might be. He used a gut leader which was fine and long. To that he attached a number-ten hook. Then he reached into his bait can, that was attached to his belt and out in front, where he carefully explored with his fingers for the right worm. He held that worm by both ends and stretched it out to full length, which did not please the worm. He reached into a vest pocket and produced a pair of small scissors. Then he snipped off one half of that worm. I was astonished,[3] since I had never read about the need of such trimming in any of the numerous books on how to catch a trout. At first I guessed that it was for economy, but not so. The technician let the right-hand half of the worm fall to the rocks, where it tied itself up, untied itself, and convulsed about, while the expert solemnly applied the left-hand half of the worm to his hook. And I con-

[2] John Milton did.
[3] And maybe the worm was.

cluded that the worm had been too long for a neat and proper bait.

He was readied: waders, creel, vest, snippers, shears, hooks, honer, net, jacket, hat, and double-vision glasses. But he waded along the brook, looking over the top of his glasses. All of this is true. And it seemed to me that my friend was cultivating the weariness of human vanity.

Surely angling for trout is a simple art, if one must call it an art. The rule and the object is to relax and loaf. And if one finds he cannot do that, he might consult someone who can tell him how to be himself, if he is credulous enough to believe that someone can.

SURETY

There is only one theory about angling in which I have perfect confidence, and this is that the two words, least appropriate to any statement about it, are the words "always" and "never."

Lord Grey of Fallodon, 1899

AND THE ENDS THEREOF

Remember that the Wit and Invention of Mankind were bestowed for other Purposes than to deceive silly Fish; and that however delightful Angling may be, it ceases to be innocent when used otherwise than as a mere Recreation.

Richard Brookes, 1766

The Sedulous

Sons of Science

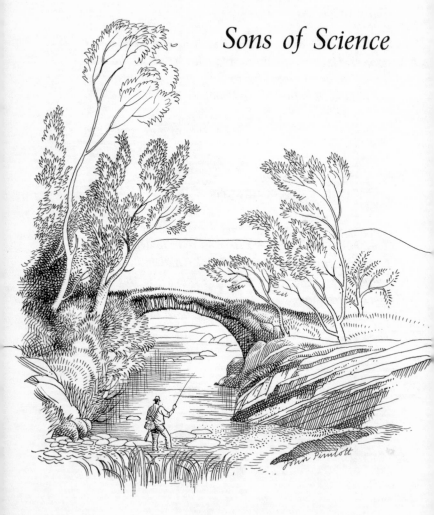

ONLY A FEW of the anglers who have read Izaak Walton's precious *The Compleat Angler* have read Captain Franck's book, *The Contemplative and Practical Angler*. I am informed that if one compares the two books on fishing one concludes that Izaak was a man of parts and, withal, a pleasant writer and that Franck's most impressive gift as an author was a flair for making the English language as weird as possible. He seems to have been a genuine genius at that.

The events of Captain[1] Franck's life are uncertain as to time and place, and if at all. He is supposed to have visited America,[2] but there isn't much in his book to sustain the supposition. However, it is assumed that this uncertain captain went to the New World once and, perhaps, once again.

Franck was a contemporary of Walton. And we have to admit that there is some evidence that he was a more adroit angler than the beloved Walton. Franck says that he met the old patron saint of anglers at Stafford. He says that they argued about the reproduction of pike. He declares that Izaak maintained that when pike appeared in waters where there had been none, the newcome pike had originated in the slime of the pickerel weed. Captain Dick Franck poohed that and tried to set Walton straight. Dick de-

[1] If he was a captain. I am indebted to a treasured friend, the late Charles E. Goodspeed, and his excellent study of Richard Franck and his books, which was published in the *Bookmen's Holiday*, 1943, for all I know about Franck. There is a sample of Franck's writing in "The Salmon's Mating," in Mr. Goodspeed's *A Treasury of Fishing Stories*, A. S. Barnes, New York, 1946.

[2] Mr. Goodspeed found a passage in Cotton Mather's Diary that he thought might have been about Richard Franck. If so, it would indicate that Franck was in Boston, Massachusetts, in 1713.

clared that the pike spawn was transferred from one pond to another on the legs of wading birds. Franck says that Walton went off in a huff.

Franck's *Practical Angler* was published in a longer book called *Northern Memoirs*, 1694. My eyes found a statement wherein the author said that he did not intend to inflict the reader "with variety of Waters, suitability of Baits; as also the making of Instruments, arming Hooks," etc cetera. He said, "For that end, you may dedicate your Opinion to what scribbling Puta-tioner[3] you please; the Complete Angler, if you will, who tells you a tedious Fly Story, extravagantly collected from antiquated Authors such as Gesner, Dubravius, &c." I was impressed. "And here," I said, "is a man who is going to write a book about the fun of fishing and fishing for the fun of it. And what a noun is *Putationer!*" Alas. What a wonderful book that would have been if Franck had told us more about the good human joy of fishing in merry England and bonnie Scotland.[4] His lore about how to fish sounds elemental or, sometimes, unessential. Instead of going on with the good project, Franck squats, as if exclaiming to himself, "What am I saying? Who gives a damn about fishing for the fun of it?" So the poor old putationer goes off in the opposite extreme, making an ass of himself, as many of his successors have done. For an example, here is Franck on worms: "But the Classis of Worms are multiform and various; manifestly the Lob, or more properly the Dew-worm, Knob or knotted Worm; Red-worm, Brandlin, Gild-tail, Marsh-worm; Flag and Dock-worm, Tag and Tagil,

[3] Franck was a connoisseur of words.
[4] He probably fished in Scotland in the year 1658.

Spotspere, Munck and Muck-worm; Cod-worm and Straw-worm, &c. But it is impossible to enumerate the innumerable[5] Sorts and Varieties of Worms, and the Texture of Insects (different also in Shape, Colour, Beauty and Proportion) except prophetically instructed beyond the due mediums of Art, or otherwise inspected by natural Observation: As when to imagine some of them smooth, of a contrary Quality are those that are ruff, fretted, and knotted."

Perhaps that is enough of worms. The passage creeps and crawls with wormy wisdom.

But Franck sometimes wrote with some sense and a bit of art—when he was not trying to impress an imaginary audience. One likes him and goes along with him when he urges anglers in his time to use light tackle, a tapered line, and sharp hooks. Sometimes he oversimplified the craft, like that old one to use bright flies for dull days and dull flies for bright days, which is so neatly and so remarkably silly. He advised the angler to "stand close" when fishing a stream, meaning that one should keep back where the fish cannot see him or his shadow. He said that the angler should keep one eye on the fish and the other on the tip of his rod, but I do not think that the captain could do that. Best of all his advice was the admonition to keep a taut line but to use no violence. And that proves that he was an angler of parts and craft. I suppose that he had the purist in mind when he said, "If the stream is muddy, try bottom fishing." So one must conclude that Franck did make an excellent point now and then, and to use one of his own garish phrases, what

[5] A prodigious task indeed. See Izaak Walton's list in *The Compleat Angler*.

more could the "Sedulous Sons of Science" want?

But best of all I like a passage wherein the garrulous old sinner[6] reveals some sentiment. Take this one: "Let us relinquish the Suburbs of *Leven*, to trace the flourishing Skirts of the *Calvin*, whose smiling Streams invite the Angler to examine them; for here one would think the Stones were steep'd in the Oil of Oespres, to invite the Fish to come ashore: where you may observe every bubbling Stream reflect a Smile on the amorous Banks, covered with Green, and enamell'd with Flowers. Here also the Sylvans upon shady Bushes bathe themselves in silver Streams; *and where Trouts do sport and divert the Angler,*[7] will leap on Shore, though with the loss of their Lives: so that if Demonstration be Truth, and Eye-Sight Evidence to convince the incredulous, there's not a Rivulet in *Scotland*, upon the angler's examination, super-excels this Calvin, for diversion with small Trout; whose translucid Streams, because so rich in themselves, and so numerous in Trouts, make them over-curious of self-preservation; for with a Rod in my Hand (but I almost blush to report it, because suspecting the incredulity of some incredulous Persons) I have ushered to those pleasant and delightful Shores, ten or twelve brace of Trouts in an Hour."[8]

[6] Franck felt that he was a devout fellow. See his *Admirable Adventures.*

[7] My italics. The only reason the Maine development boys have not borrowed that string of words is that they haven't read Franck's book.

[8] From *Northern Memoirs,* as quoted by Charles E. Goodspeed in *Bookmen's Holiday,* The New York Public Library, 1943.

LET THE TRUTH BE TOLD

I caught my last trout with a worm.
               Piscator, in The Compleat Angler

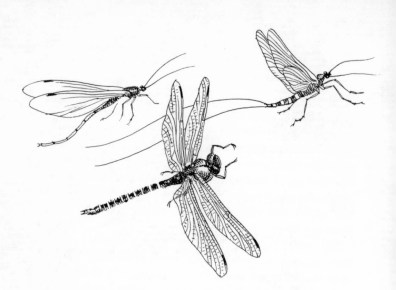

Trout Eat This and That

How SIMPLE IS the worm fisherman. He gets up early in the morning to dig for worms. The dew is on the primrose by the river's brim, but he digs for worms. And with his angleworms he expects to beguile a creature that lives off the fat of the land, the water, and the air. I learned when a small boy that sometimes one must unlearn what he has learned. One of the old errors was that angleworms were best for catching trout.

The right bait for catching trout is some of what they happen to be eating *or something like it*. The only reason that I know for the popularity of the angleworm[1] is that it is often easily obtained and that it stays on a hook, once so arranged. But there are numerous baits for trout. Crickets are good bait, although crickets are fragile—and I like crickets. Grasshoppers are better bait for trout, but they are full of molasses.

The point right now is that trout eat this and that. Once, during an hour of recollection, I wrote a story that I called "The Big Trout of Stand Up Rips." And in that tale the big trout was caught by a dangler who could stoop to bait his hook with a small hoptoad.

The letter-writing fraternity went after me when that story was published. Most of them made the same brilliant point. They asserted dogmatically that a trout would not eat a toad because a toad exudes a milky poison which is so disagreeable that only a snake can take it. I was challenged as a fisherman and as a naturalist with emphasis on the point that I wasn't

[1] Among fishermen.

either one or the other. I had to admit that I had not
tasted a toad. But who knows how a toad tastes to a
trout. The toad of Stand Up Rips was a small toad, a
baby rained-down toad. Perhaps such a toad tastes like
a marshmallow in a trout's mouth.

But all that speculation and assertion were silly, because there was history behind that story. The big
trout of Stand Up Rips did swallow a toad, and it was
thus that he came to his ignoble end, and so, maybe,
will the fellow who baited his hook with that toad. I
confess that I do not know what toad among the toads
that toad was. Maybe it was a wee specimen of *Bufo
americanus*. Perhaps it represented *Bufo fowleri*, best
it could. Toads look like toads to me. And toads look
like toads to trout, I dare say. And trout are not dis-
criminating feeders as a rule.

At one time or another trout will eat anything that
moves about where trout are hungry and on the
prowl. A trout will eat newts, spotted newts, two-lined
newts, dusky newts, or any other "lizard" that comes
his way. A trout will eat bloodsuckers. A trout will eat
a hellbender. Trout will eat mice. In fact, and this is
a fact, a trout will eat anything that creeps, crawls,
scuttles, swims, sinks, flutters, flies, or jets. Our brook
trout, splendid *Salvelinus fontinalis*, is a prodigious
feeder when the signs and the seasons are sumptuous.
And therefore he is as full of vitamins as an August
cricket.

AS DUD SAID

If I knew all erbout fishin' fer trout, I w'ud give it up and tackle sunthin' more int'resting.

Dud Dean

John Pimlott

Matchsticks and So On

TROUT ARE SOMETIMES promiscuous feeders, but one can not get at this all in one flat statement. One needs to consider it and various data. For instance, here on my desk lies a folder that is printed in twenty-eight colors. There are not that many colors, but there are on this folder because it displays flies—dry flies, wet flies, streamer flies, and bucktail flies. Of course this folder is designed to sell another book about how to catch trout with flies. And according to this folder there are more than two hundred fly patterns printed

in their true colors in this new book. Moreover, there are eight hundred additional black-and-white prints. That seems to add up to more than one thousand flies. This wonderful book about flies and how to fish with flies sells for only twenty dollars a copy in the plain edition for the *hoi polloi*. There is a fifty-dollar-per-copy edition for the reckless or affluent. I have been near to buying a copy of the trade edition, and I may before I lose the folder, although the folder may be worth as much as the book. But I only intended to say that such books are published year after year. People buy them. And that proves that there is a would-be angler born every minute. But men who go down to the river to fish with a fly are bound to suffer more than one confounding.

Good yesterday, I fished from a commodious rowboat. I enjoy the spaciousness of a flat-bottomed rowboat from which one may fish as he pleases. I kindled my pipe and tossed the match away, as one may do when he is sure that the match will land in a thousand acres of rain water. But I had not counted on the show that followed. Swirl, splash! A big and handsome trout struck at the matchstick. He hit it vigorously. And he spat it out vigorously. I have seen that happen before. Why had the big trout charged at the matchstick? Does a matchstick look like an insect or some small fish?[1]

It is often said that few flies closely imitate the insect or whatever the designer had for a model. They mean that few flies resemble an insect so much as a matchstick resembles a matchstick.[2] When I was a small boy, and more interested in catching trout than in reading about how to catch trout, I heard a man who was eighty years old tell a man who was seventy-five years old that once upon a time he stopped his horse on a bridge over a small country brook. And he saw several trout in the June brook water under that bridge. He had always made it a practice, so he said, to carry a line and hooks in his buggy,[3] but he couldn't find worms, crickets, grasshoppers, or any suitable bait. Then he saw a small bush that was

---

[1] A friend of mine declares that he tied a long shanked hook on a matchstick and then caught a big male trout with a cigar butt in his stomach.

[2] Un-huh.

[3] Perhaps the time has come when one should explain that a *buggy* was a wagon and that a wagon was a four-wheeled rig to hitch behind a horse. As for a horse, see an encyclopedia.

adorned with bright red berries. And he decided to try one of those red berries. And he caught all the trout he wanted with those red berries for bait.

If the guess is right, those berries were the fruit of the black ash bush, and they are insipid to my taste. Did those trout think that those berries looked like an egg sac? What did those trout think that those berries were? Or must we decide that trout do not think? However, the matchstick and the red berries were provocatives, that is, they did lure the trout. When trout are hungry, they are voracious. Perhaps it follows that the lure need only simulate[4] what a trout usually takes to be food. So we may conclude that a trout samples many things, which, if they prove to be unpalatable, the trout rejects before a boy could say, "I've got a nibble."

So the origin of artificial flies was simple. A bird on the wing drops a feather on a pond where a fisherman pensively floats in a birch-bark canoe. The feather floats.[5] A current of air stirs the feather. And up comes a trout to hit at it. Or a damsel fly struts on the gunnel of the crude canoe. The fisherman idly brushes it aside. The damsel fly is surprised and upside down. It kicks about in the water where it sprawls. A trout rises and devours it. Or to suppose a third and more urgent situation, a worm fisherman sits through a hatch of winged creatures that must first abide a wingless state in the bottom murks of pond or lake or stream. Before this hatch of flies the trout have been as unapparent as the May flies, but when the airy creatures begin to hatch, the trout ap-

[4] Izaak Walton said, "Counterfeit."
[5] Also pensively.

pear everywhere, to feed with mad abandon. Yet not a trout will touch the fisherman's worms on his carefully baited hook. In such ways men learned to make lures and flies. Why bother with such as worms, when trout will strike at a floating feather, a red berry, or a pine matchstick?

ON A BRILLIANT NIGHT IN JUNE

In a bowl to sea went wise men three,
On a brilliant night in June:
They carried a net, and their hearts were set
On fishing up the moon.

Thomas Love Peacock, "The Wise Men of Gotham"

'Tis an affair of luck.

Henry Van Dyke, Fisherman's Luck

Angling may be said to be so like mathematics
that it can never be fully learnt.

Preface, The Compleat Angler

More About Matchsticks

and So On

I FISHED with an accomplished angler up in the western end of Ellis Pond. The day and the weather were at odds. The sky was full of wind and wet, but now and then the sun smudged through. There were times when the lake was as blue as in better days, but for the rest of it, the water was an unfriendly drab as if it were in the mood to drown someone. Such a setting for fishing looked like bad luck, and it had been for me, although I was casting my flies with particular care. And I had changed flies when tried patterns failed after a reasonable chance and trial. I did not catch one trout, but all that while my friend, the angler, hooked twenty or more and set them free.

I continued to fish without a rise. After enduring the situation, I decided to ask my friend what fly he was using, what magical fly brought him such fortune, while I fished on *sans* trout. I found that it was not easy to ask Ken the question, because I had stuffed it out so long with the thought, "I'll get them yet." So I had to assemble each word and then labor to keep my voice casual.

"What fly are you using?"

Ken had been fishing wet, just as I had, but when he swung around to show me the extraordinary fly, it was only a number ten *dry* fly of an undistinguished grayness. I think that Ken may have considered the pattern was important because he said that it had worked as well ten days before. But I quickly discovered that the pattern did *not* matter, if the fly was about the same size and color and one fished it the way Ken was abusing his. That is, he was casting that fly toward the shore as far as he could, and then he was bringing it back as one does a wet fly, on the surface. And the fly, so managed, rolled, skittered, and hopped ridiculously. But for some reason of the moment in the history of Ellis Pond, the trout thought that a dry fly fished in that unholy way was an alluring morsel.

There are hours when obscure factors contrive to make fishing with a fly a whimsical adventure. Twenty years ago Bunny Pierce and I went fishing from a rowboat in Cold Stream Pond. The early evening was one of those twilights when the big May flies hatch and hatch. There were thousands of trout feeding on the surface of that beautiful lake, but not one of them had so much as spat at the various flies we had offered them. We changed flies and changed flies. And we fished and fished. Near the end of that prolonged hatch Bunny put on a Marabou streamer fly. I smiled indulgently at the trial. It proved to be useless when fished in a conventional manner, but when Bunny permitted the big fly to sink, and then pulled it up with rapid jerks, a big trout hit it mightily. I got out a Marabou in a hurry. And we caught twenty handsome trout while the last of the twilight went over to the night and the stars.

We thought that Bunny had a solution. Just take a white Marabou, let it sink, pull it upward as if a nymph were rising to hatch. I wrote a story about it. Then came disillusionment. We tried the White Marabou many times when May flies were hatching, but it failed to do that trick again, that is, with any particular success. Why did the Marabou "work" so excellently and then fail us when circumstances seemed to be much the same? Was our success at Cold Stream Pond because of a circumstance of light on the water or in the water? Perhaps. All I know is that too often what was only whimsy and chance has been mistaken for dependable lore.

Trout are usually finicky[1] during an abundant hatch or swarming of May flies. We all have memories of times when the water "boiled" with feeding trout that were indifferent to the flies we cast them. At Rock Pond, 5, Range 6, I fished out an evening

[1] *Finicky* seems a better word for piscatorial records than fastidious or any other synonym.

when the trout were rising everywhere on the surface, but exclusively. I noticed that among the large, handsome May flies were yellow specimens. The trout were catching the traditional gray May flies as eagerly as the yellow, but the yellow variation reminded me of a yellow pop bug that I had in my pack. The body was a deep yellow. The head was red. The wings were a nondescript brown, tied closely to the body. It did not look like a May fly, but it was dominantly yellow and it floated.

I cast it. And a pound-and-a-quarter trout, with a belly as red as a red tulip, slashed up and down on the bass bug. And from that time until pitch-black dark I hooked too many trout from anyone's point of view, and most of those sightly trout came up clear of the water to strike that lure head-down. That was spectacular trouting. And, once more, I was sure that I had a sure way to catch trout during a hatch of May flies. It does work once in a while. More often it does not.

LIGHTER OR SADDER

About the making of flies: "and upon any occasion vary, and make them lighter or sadder, according to your fancy, or the day."

Piscator, in The Compleat Angler

The Fly a Little Girl Tied

I KNEW at a glance that the little girl had tied an impossible fly. But the little girl was as winsome and as sweet as the early morning in May when the bluebirds come back to Maine for the summer. And she had tied the fly for me. How much I wish I had been less the critic and more like the little girl, for of such is the goodness of life as well as the Kingdom of Heaven.

"Sister" had wrapped the long shank of an ungainly number eight hook with green store twine, and the wings of that fly had been cut from the wings of a Thanksgiving turkey. Those wings were as blunt and stiff as an old maid's upper lip. So for a long time the fly lay in the pen tray on my desk. It stayed there until the little girl had grown up and gone off to college and then to be married. And when she was too busy to tie flies, I looked at that forlornly clumsy fly, and in me there was a surge of emotion, and I said, "I'm going to catch a fish of some sort on that fly or give up fishing." It was silly. I knew it for such. There had been a time when the little girl would have been delighted if I had caught a trout on her fly, but that was long ago.

I took the fly to the Kennebec River, which flows on the west edge of our town. And there at the river that evening I met the usual expert. And he told me, "They are mighty choosy tonight. And they won't look at anything bigger than a number fourteen—sixteen would be better."

What if I had showed him the fly the little girl had tied? It is probable that he would have gone uptown with the news that Mak Macdougall had gone bughouse. Well, I was going to fish with a purpose in mind other than the expert knows. And I said, "Dry flies be hanged." And with lifted eyebrows the expert went home, where he was not an expert.

I tied on the little girl's fly. When wet, the green ebbed out of the twine until it was a gray. And it cast, as I had guessed it would, with a triggy feeling. And I did not catch a trout with it on the first cast or the second. But I had foreseen all that, except the fading of the green twine. So I fished with pleasant memories. And as I fished, the day passed, and a grayness settled over the river, and a small south wind began to blow in my face.

We have long known that when a south wind blows up the Kennebec the barometric pressure is falling and the trout seek cover and safety. So there I was, fishing with an impossible fly, that Thanksgiving-turkey fly, while a stormy wind blew steadily up the river.

I have no right to go on with this. All the wise lads in the world who have fished with a fly are only waiting for me to tell the probable truth and to shut up. But, brother, let us thank God that the truth sometimes happens to confound the wise and prudent. A salmon rose up out of that gray water, smelling the south wind as he came, and he bashed that fly. He was not a large salmon among his kind, but he was a vigorous, slithering fighting organism. And, as "Sister" would have said when she tied that fly, he hooked his own self. For my guess, he weighed about three pounds and was about six years old. I caught him on the fly a little girl had tied, so I put him back in the river.

But that was not the end of it. Within half an hour I caught a fat half-pound trout, a gorgeous thing. And it was evident that she would have something to do with the trout population in the Kennebec, so I disengaged the crude hook with the brittle old wings of turkey feather. That seemed to be the thing to do with that trout: let her go back to the river. The little girl would have liked it that way.

A TIME FOR EVERY PURPOSE

For everything there is a season, and a time for every purpose under heaven: a time to be born, and a time to die; a time to plant, and a time to pluck up that which is planted; a time to kill, and a time to heal; a time to break down, and a time to build up; a time to weep, and a time to laugh; a time to mourn, and a time to dance; a time to cast away stones, and a time to gather stones together; a time to embrace, and a time to refrain from embracing; a time to seek, and a time to lose; a time to keep, and a time to cast away; a time to rend, and a time to sew; a time to keep silence, and a time to speak; a time to love, and a time to hate; a time for war, and a time for peace.

Ecclesiastes 3:1–8

How to Fish
the Wrong Way Right

I sold my first fishing story to *Field and Stream.*
And that was many years ago. And during all the
years that I wrote for that excellent magazine I did
not discover any doubt in the minds of the editor and
his associates of the magazine's excellency. Even its
subscribers subscribed to that opinion.

Once during those years I wrote a story which I
called "Up Along the Baker." But when it was sold
to *Field and Stream* it was a revamped story. Nevertheless, the first version was a truthful report of fishing down Baker Stream. I worked carefully to describe that magnificent wilderness valley through
which Baker Stream flows from Rock Pond to Baker
Flowage. And I had caught trout all the way for six
miles, trout that weighed from a half pound or so to
three pounds. So I had something to write about. And,
by the way, I caught those trout on dry flies that I
fished *down* the stream all the way. That departure
from the usual dry-fly technique began with the fact
that those trout would not take, or pay any attention
to, my wet flies. I will tell you about the rest of it
in a moment.

Ray P. Holland was editor.[1] And I think that he

[1] Ray P. Holland was editor of *Field and Stream* from 1924–1941.
He is now writing his own stories and books.

was the most able of the editors who gunned the out-door magazines at that time. He was a big, tall, raw-boned fellow who knew his stuff from A to Z. He had learned his book in the field. And he was an able writer. I do not think that Holland questioned my honesty when I wrote about fishing dry flies down-stream with extravagant success. That was all right with Ray P. Holland. But, of course, in the book the veriest novice knew that one fished dry flies *up* the stream and not *down* the stream. That was the only way one could properly manage a dry fly.

Now of course Mr. Holland did not explain why he rejected that story in the first place. But I know now that if he had published it as I wrote it he would have been lettered under by subscribers and newsstand customers. They would have written, all of them, "Dry flies are fished *up*stream. Wet flies are fished *down*stream." And a few subscribers might have can-celed their subscriptions. And that would have been too much. All editors are careful of subscriptions. In fact, an editor would cheerfully cancel a subscriber to save a subscription.

So my story came home. But I had written truth-fully. I told it all as it happened. When I began the trip down the Baker, I offered my stock of wet flies. But the trout—and I saw them—refused to rise to my wet flies. Then I tried a small dry fly that was invented by Roy Barrows. He called it the Stratford. It worked like magic going down the Baker.

You see, the trout were at the foot of the pools and runs that day, and I took them on fairly long casts, floating the fly no more than a yard or so. I caught more than one hundred trout that afternoon. And they were big, handsome fellows. Moreover, I have since caught trout that way many a time. And I shouldn't be surprised if an article such as that one about fishing with a dry fly down Baker Stream failed to evoke "So what?" these days.

It isn't bright to dogmatize about trout fishing. Flies are only the trouter's means to an end. And there are times when one must know how to do the wrong thing the right way. And that reminds me of another story that was rejected. It was about a remarkable Irish setter bitch. It was a pleasure to tell that story, because she was a patrician, a queen of Irish setters. But that Irish setter whelped a litter of black pups. They were black when they were born. So they were black from start to finish.

In the story the bitch appeared for what she was, a most intelligent gun dog, willing, smart, and accomplished. As I liked it, the bitch's abilities made the story. The pups were only incidental in the story, and I only mentioned them because two of them grew up to be almost as clever in the field as their mother was. It was a good hunting story. I know it was because I have read scores of hunting stories, and most of them only went "Bang, bang!" But the story did *not* sell. The editors said, "For your information, Irish setters are red. They are not black."

I had not said that the black pups were Irish setters. Their mother was, with papers a mile long, impeccable and unimpeachable. But of course the boys who write letters to the editors would have grabbed their pens and typewriters with glee if that story had been published. They would have said, "Doesn't that fool writer of yours know that Irish setters do not have black pups?" Alas, even the red setter bitch knew that her pups should have been red.

But I did fish down the Baker with dry flies. And I did catch trout all the way. And that handsome Irish setter did have black pups. Furthermore, Ecclesiastes said about three thousand years ago that there is a time for everything. A time to do this, and a time to do that. And I venture to add that there is also a time to do the wrong thing the right way.

But I do not mean to dogmatize about black pups.

AND SOME LEMONS

You are to know that there are so many sorts of flies as there be of fruits.

The Compleat Angler

The Best Fly Is Not Yet

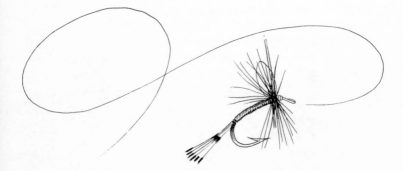

IZAAK WALTON WROTE, "You ought to note that there are twelve kinds of artificial, made flies, to angle with upon the top of the water." Now there are four thousand and seven hundred flies.[1] Who names all the flies by name these days? Some are named from their originators. Some are called so and so of the material of which they are made, as is the Marabou. Or a fly may come by its name suspiciously, promiscuously, or profanely.

The most successful flies are those that somehow resemble common foods on a trout's menu. Other flies may resemble seasonal or rarely taken foods. Either way, the fly must look devourable from a trout's-eye point of view. Therefore, when one buys flies, he should try to feel the way a trout feels when he is hungry. And we need to remember that there are more bugs in the earth, the air, and the water than are contained in our private entomologies.[2] Moreover, the region where one fishes may turn up its exigencies. Perhaps a trout might let a fly go past because it looked too much like a nymph or insect he had never seen. Perhaps?

Fishing is the way to learn to fish with a fly and a fly. Now and then fishermen get excited about a fly that has been "outlawed" in England or the Sahara Desert. That fly is said to be a wicked killer or an irresistible lure. But all the "outlawed" flies that I have seen in my time proved to be fifth-raters. The Alexandra (wet) was one of those "deadly" patterns.

[1] Not a careful count.
[2] By arrangement with an old-time fisherman who angled on Avon and said, "There are more things in heaven and earth, Horatio, than are dreamt of in our philosophy."

The word went about that it was prohibited by law
in England. That pretty fly could not be used in England's waters. No, sir! One understood that if a man
used that Alexandra fly in England he would be hung
until he was dead and then buried outside Westmin-
ster Abbey. Now all of this may backfire on me. Perhaps the Alexandra is an illegal fly in England, if
there are any illegal flies in England. I can only say
that it isn't a dangerous fly in this neck of the woods.

Some of our trained biologists in the service of
Maine have reported that their tests and checks show
that a fly fisherman takes more fish in a season than
a bait fisherman. For a moment one almost yields to
that old-fashioned flattery, but it is my opinion that
those gentlemen need instruction in the gentle art,
because a bait fisherman can trim any fly fisherman
that comes down the brook, even if he fishes up the
brook again. I mean day in and day out the season
long. Furthermore, it is not true that a wet-fly fisherman will take more trout than a dry-fly angler. Times
and seasons level off all fishermen. And for that reason I shall not take sides.

I have been most often a wet-fly fisherman, but I
admire dry flies and the art of using them. Some of
my friends tie dry flies that are incredibly neat and
artistic. They are good enough to be embedded in
crystal.[3] And some of the best fellows I know are dry-
flyers pure and simple. In fact, they are determined
to fish 'em dry wherever and whenever, and to the
devil with it, but I long ago learned that there is no
more virtue in them than there is in wormers.

I once wasted a rare forenoon in June with a

[3] I mean the flies.

preacher of the Gospel who seemed to think that the twelve apostles were dry-fly purists. And he stubbornly, self-righteously, and slavishly refused to try wet flies when his dry flies failed. Therefore it was unfortunate for him that I had planned to fish down Austin Stream, since to leave me and to fish up the stream would have advanced him into the wilderness and away from the car and our base of supplies.

He solved his dilemma this way: by walking down the stream about one hundred yards. Then he fished up that stretch while I waited at the starting place. He did not propose that I wait for him, but my part seemed to be indicated in the procedure. So when the man fished up to me without so much as an old-fashioned nibble, he walked down the stream about two hundred yards, while I began to fish down the first one hundred yards. It was a performance, and if the fellow had not been recognized as a prodigious brain, I should have suspected that he wasn't.

But he was bound to grow weary of that plan, if for no other reason than that he didn't find any trout, and at last when he met me, gleaning after his dry flies, he said, with a hard look on his ascetic face, "This is a waste of time. There are no trout in this brook."

It so happened that even as he spoke a trout came up at my old Dark Montreal in a fussy, spitty manner. I saw that trout and the golden splash of water where he missed the fly, and I know that preacher saw that trout. But when I asked him, "Did you see that trout?" he replied, "I didn't see anything much."

Let us hope that I was genuinely humble[4] when

[4] Knowing full well that I was not.

I opened the lid of my creel and when I held a trout under his nose and also pointed at six more. And what did the preacher say? He said, "Huh, I didn't think that you would stoop to worming them."

But let us conclude all this talk about fishing with flies and flies. I have caught more salmon with a Black Ghost streamer than with any other fly. And the Gray Ghost comes next. But have I caught more salmon with the Black and Gray Ghost streamers because they are superior, as lures, or because I have spent more time fishing with them than with other patterns? May we conclude that an angler will catch more fish with the fly he uses most? And if we knew all about fishing for trout, would not we give it up for something more interesting?

ABOUT SKUNK HUNTING
MOONLIGHT NIGHTS

All of a sudden, the blessed quietness was sp'iled by that dog. But Misty was real pleased. He beamed in the moonlight. "This," he says, "is a danged fine night. He's found another one."

Maybe the skunk thought it was a nice night. Thar he was, standing his ground, unperturbable, as the poet says. I didn't need to hold the lantern fer Misty. He strode in calm as a clam. In a twinkle, he had that skunk by the tail. It kinda pawed with its front feet, but Misty dropped him in the sack careless as all-git-in-trouble. The procedure was always the same. The dog stopped his circlin' when Misty stepped in fer the skunk, but he barked louder than ever. While the skunk watched the dog, Misty did the rest. That c'ud git tiresome, but not unless yer fergot how fraught with danger it was.

From "The Skunk King"

Certain

Uncertain

Certainties

THIS IS NOT about old man Greene and his famous skunk dog—that is, not so much about them as about the uncertain certainties. At this tick of the clock, when the sputniks are beeping back at us like frightened and homesick things in orbits not to their liking, there is an urgent human need to be wary about too much "scientific" certainty. Yet it is now a heresy to be unscientific and to question the certainties, because it is presumed that it is our destiny to be the lords of all we want to survey.

Old man Greene had a famous skunk dog. I do not know how many breeds he was, and I cannot describe him after all the years between. I did hear it said that the dog was part wire-haired terrier and some bull-dog. Whatever, he was a small dog and every inch the skunk dog.

If someone wants to know why anyone would want to go skunk hunting, perhaps I should explain that this belongs back in that time in the history of the United States when six dollars was an important sum of money and that a black skunk was worth six dollars, which was also worth six dollars in an exchange of goods. The short-striped skunk was only worth four dollars, and a narrow-striped skunk was only worth two dollars,[1] while a broad-striped skunk was only worth an old-fashioned American dollar.

That was the easiest part to explain. Money was money, but folks needed it. There were other inducements and enticements, as the young fellow said when he married a good-looking heiress. First, there were the imponderable affairs of the night that a

[1] In other words, that was as much as a big day's pay for a laborer.

young man feels but can't talk about.[2] And the sharp, frosty, tangy nights are most intriguing. Second, there was that sense of being off from the humdrum to the adventurous. Even when the risk and hazard were only that one might run into a barbed-wire fence or fall down a forgotten and uncovered well, there was an exhilaration about going hunting for skunks. It was a nocturnal affair.

Old man Greene's dog had a system. We thought it was unbeatable. Or perhaps that isn't fair. Perhaps some parts of the system were old man Greene's. Prime skunks were valuable skunks. But "blue" skunks went for half the money or less than that. "Prime" meant long, thick fur and a white pelt. "Blue" meant unprime, inferior fur and a dark, discolored pelt.

Cold weather primes fur and pelt, but skunks are most abroad and active before the cold weather begins. September is their busy month where old man Greene lived. Then they are out to fatten themselves before the long sleeps during the harsher winter months. Therefore it was easier to find skunks before they were prime. On that assignment old man Greene and his dog were a team. They caught skunks all through the early falltime. The old man brought them home alive, shut them up in pens and coops, fed them all they could eat, and pelted them when they were prime.

But the dog invented the *modus operandi*. Old man Greene and his disciples followed the dog. We often

[2] Walt Whitman tried and he came close to communicating this sense of the infinity of the night to his fellow men. See "Night on the Prairie."

walked ten miles from dark to gray morning. The dog traveled around the mowing fields and pastures. When he found a busy skunk, he walked around and around the animal, barking slowly and provocatively. It was a simple stunt. The circulatory pace, unhurried, and seemingly measured and timed, bewildered the skunk, which faced the dog, rear guns elevated as it were, and kept facing the dog as the dog slowly circled his skunk.

The dog was always calm and deft. While the skunk watched the dog, turning as the dog went around, the old man walked in and grasped the skunk by its tail and quickly lifted it off the ground. Then one of his sons would hold a grain sack open, and that skunk was in the bag. After that the disoriented creature could be lugged anywhere.

It was old man Greene's conviction that a skunk lifted off all four feet could not. And his neighbors and all who had witnessed those performances were convinced that it was so. So the "scientific" theory was that a suspended skunk was a disempowered skunk. We were sure of it. Had we not seen it demonstrated again and again? It was a certainty.

But one night, an almost white night, when we "could see as well as in the daytime," that beautiful certainty became an other than. At first all went as usual, or we supposed that all was as usual. But how underhanded a turn of events can be. Round and round barked the old dog. With black small eyes the skunk kept pace from inside the circle. And old man Greene flat-footed into the arena. There was no fumble. The old man lifted the broad-striped skunk off his feet quickly and confidently. But before the young fellow who had the bag could get there, that skunk did what skunks cannot do when suspended off all fours. But old man Greene did not let go. He was wrapped in a thick cloud of skunk. It repeated and repeated while the brave old man held on, shouting, "Leo! Sam! You! The bag, the bag!"

That was a profoundly disturbing experience. And that night I saw a certainty get lost like a speck of fluff in the Milky Way.

LARKIN RODS

Sometime in some story I told about how I came by my first fly rod. After that a multimillionaire wrote to me—the only communication I ever had with "cold millions." The man wrote, "You say that your first rod was a Larkin premium rod, earned by selling Larkin products from house to house. So was mine. And it was the best rod I ever possessed. By the way, that took a lot of selling. And I am wondering if you have missed your calling. Any boy who could sell enough Larkin soaps and stuff to get a fly rod should have grown up to be tops as a salesman—in fact, I did."

That was the end of the letter from the multimillionaire and the end of our correspondence. But it all goes to prove that any American boy who could earn a Larkin rod might end up a millionaire or a preacher.

Rods and Rods

IF ONE DOES not know how to catch a trout, he should not consult an ordinary variety of fisherman, because such a person is so uncomplicated as to be of no scientific or technical help. Some of those ordinary trouters talk about "fish poles." Of course they mean *rods*. That is, they refer to rods as "fish poles." In fact, I once heard one of those fellows speak of a "fly pole," and, brother, that is the end. The term rod, or fly rod, is precise. One means a *rod*, and one does not mean a pole. You may go on voting as you usually vote, or you may split the ticket, or you may even swap parties, but you must not call a fly rod a *pole*. That, sir, is not done. One cannot deny that tons of trout have been caught with poles, but a pole is a pole, and it is only a pole.

But what is a rod? Izaak Walton had rods made of fir wood, greenheart, or something. What else? I do not know. He plunges off the subject into talk about flies, lines, and baits, as if these accessories were of any use without a rod. One is almost provoked to yell at Walton and Charles Cotton, "Hold on, gentlemen. What about rods, rods, *rods?*" On the other hand, latter-day writers of how-to and where-to books have devoted too much space to rods and rods. Indeed, after one has read those dreary pages on how rods are made and should be made, unmade and revarnished, his mind easily turns to thoughts of poles, just poles, with considerable pleasure.

Perhaps the most puzzling advice on how to choose your rod is found in *The Compleat Angler*. Quote: "For the length of your rod must always be governed by the breadth of the river you may choose to angle at: and for a Trout-river, one five or six yards long is commonly enough; and longer, though never so neatly and artificially made, it ought not to be, if you intend to fish at ease; and if otherwise, where lies the sport?"

Six times three are eighteen. That is, if a yard was a yard in Walton's day.[1] Eighteen feet is more than a rod, and a rod is a perch or a pole. No wonder persons are confused on this subject. Moreover, although Walton says that the length of your rod is governed by the width of the river, not a thing is said about the length of your line being governed by the length of the river, yet one might logically expect something of the sort.

I have been looking in the Encyclopaedia Britannica, fourteenth edition. What does this source have to say about rods? I cannot find anything under "Rods" about rods. Of course it is possible that they have somthing to say about rods under "P" (for poles, etc.). Under "Rod," they tell us about Edouard Rod, who was a Swiss novelist until 1910. After Edouard Rod the book rambles off into *Rodentis,* which is "an order of placentia mammals characterized by the peculiar front incisor teeth, which are reduced to a sin-

[1] In England a yard is a yard when the temperature is 62 degrees F. Otherwise it might be more or it might be less.

gle functional pair in each jaw, specially adapted to gnawing, and growing throughout life." A man might envy these creatures whose teeth replenish themselves as they wear, but such information isn't much help when one is trying to educate himself on the subject of rods.

I count as my friends good fellows who have an almost endless source of information and talk about rods. They own many. And each rod has its history, where it was made, by whom it was made, and, endlessly, *how* it was made. So much talk is frightening. One gets in a frame of mind wherein he dare not buy a rod, lest it prove to be the wrong rod or less a rod than some other rod. And in such a state of nerves and mind the simple, elemental fact—namely, that fellows who work in reliable stores, specializing in fishing equipment, might know *something* about the rods they sell and be able to select the rod one needs—is forgotten. If one told them where he expected to fish, for the most part, and what he hoped to catch, these fellows who handle rods all their lives, and who talk with men who make and sell rods all their lives, might be trusted.

After all, manufacturers of rods have made excellent progress. The modern rod is a careful and precise instrument. And I would not make much more of a mystery of it than that. Of course, our fly rods are works of art that deserve acclaim. Izaak Walton would be astonished at the modern rod. With a rod, picked from any one of the reputable makes, and a nice line to fit it, a novice could stand in the middle of a river and then cast several times farther than Izaak could.

I know men who build their own rods. But before a man who wants to fish, rather than to build rods, undertakes to make a rod, he should examine the cross sections from a few well-made rods. Those sections of bamboo are fitted so nicely that the glue is squeezed. And the parts, six or eight, are cut so precisely that they fit to the heart of the rod. Rods are the product of precision and nice tools.

Don't worry about the rod. Walk into a reliable store. Buy your rod and line. To get off fishing is the thing. With a good rod, and a line and reel to match it, anyone can learn to fly fish in an hour's time, providing he has a patient friend to show him the tricks. Or if a new man is particularly attentive he can learn to fly fish in a half hour. But then he will go on learning so long as he fishes for trout.

AND NO TROUT

" '*By crotch,*' *I says,* '*I sh'ud think that ye'd hate to live away down thar.*'

" '*Why? What d'ye mean?*' *he says, kinda taken aback.*

" '*Down to N'York,*' *I says.*

" '*Why?*' *he says, like he was completely puzzled.*

" '*Becuz,*' *I says,* '*it's so far away from everything.*'

"*Then he begun to laugh, like what I'd said was funny. Now what in the devil was he laughin' at?*"

"*Search me,*" *I said.*

"*Me, too,*" *concluded Mat.*

"*Business Is Business*"

Of Ponds and Lakes

and Men

WHAT IS A POND? What is a lake? What is a sea? I think that I know an important distinction. When an angler cannot see the far shore on a clear day, that body of water is not a pond, and by my notion of what a lake should be, it is not a lake.

Shore lines, country, and hills about are part of a pond or lake. Surely water alone, even great volumes of it, does not make a pond or lake. The place, the environment, top and bottom, make a pond or a lake. The shores and country around about are the distinctive facts about a pond. Such environment makes the pond or lake memorable.

Take one big pond for an example of what I mean. For thirty-six years I have known men, talked with men, and traded letters with men who knew the wilderness greatness of Pierce Pond. Their encomiums differed in fervor and in meaning and depth according to the man. And I thought that a man's appreciation of Pierce Pond was as that man felt in his own heart. But each man felt, in his own way, the sum to-

tal of Pierce Pond. Verily there was a fraternity of us who enjoyed Pierce Pond.

Of course our eyes do not see a lake in the same light time after time. There is always some difference of cloud and water, light and wind, or windlessness. But all the while, season after season, the pond or the lake sustains a character and totality that is that pond or lake. So a lake is an affair of water and the round-abouts and even the up-aboves.

The wholeness is good for the man who is too easily divided against himself. I must admit that the water in a man's beloved lake is such as to drown him or his friends as quickly and as thoroughly as in any other pond. And I have seen the water in Pierce Pond as wild and tempestuous when lashed by wind and storm as any inland lake could be. Gull Rock is washed and scoured from top to bottom every fall and spring. The ledges at the dam have withstood spectacular and merciless poundings. And there are occasional days up there that are so cold a man out fishing becomes a lump of flesh whose only function is to endure. Surely Pierce Pond is not to be held in one's lap like an easily tamed creature!

But what of that? One learns that it is a wizardly lake wherein all creatures grow to be larger than their norm. The water and the bottom, and I do not know what else, are magic, actually so. Then there are the hills and all the neighbor ponds—those other fabulous ponds.[1] All in all, the environment is the home of Pierce Pond. They all belong. It all belongs.

The man who fishes comes to enjoy and to be inspired by many inland lakes. And because of long

[1] High and Helen, the Otter Ponds, the Kilgores, Grass Pond, etc.

acquaintance and profound delights he remembers some one pond or lake more ardently than any other. And that brings me to the heart of my conviction that there is an essential goodness in away-from-town, where there is wilderness and trout water. For all men must learn to achieve some great and vital sublimation; to make some goodness in reality their own in exchange for a lesser and, perhaps, perilous object of desire.

I am instructed that culture and its arts offer many healthy blessings in whose sublimations we can be rid of the insufficient that had us, as it were, by the throat. But culture is itself a *tour de force*. And many of us men are not adept. In my house there is a recording called "Classical Music for People Who Hate Classical Music." It has been good for me, because I am slow of mind and spirit in appreciation of classical music. I have listened faithfully to this record, and parts of it stir me, please me, or lift me up on a rock, like "Excerpt from Piano Concerto No. 1 in B-Flat Minor, Op. 23, Tchaikovsky," and "Finlandia, Tone Poem, Sibelius." But I must confess, if I tell the truth, that much of classical music disturbs me unpleasantly and therefore does not help *me*. For example, there are several places in the music of this recording of "Classical Music for People Who Hate Classical Music" where it seems to my ears that a prehistoric cow is lifting her head in the stillness to moo at Adam and Eve.

I am only saying that I think men must sometimes seek a sublimation in that which is other than culture and its arts. There are times in human living when a *tour de force* is the wrong resource. And I think that the going out, the coming back, and the being out trout fishing have been blessèd unto me. And I believe that this great experiential resource is more important than all else that gets named as a resource. Therefore I venture a prophecy that in the new and wiser days men who have learned this lesson will rise up, not in wrath, but by the urgency, to eliminate all the despoilers. If they will not learn, they must be restrained.

AND THEY SHALL BE HEALED

Now as they went on their journey, they came at eventide to the Tigres, and they lodged there. But the young man went down to wash himself, and a fish leaped out of the river, and would have swallowed up the young man. But the angel said unto him, Take a hold on the fish. And the young man caught hold of the fish, and cast him up on the land. And the angel said unto him, Cut the fish open, and take the heart and the liver and the gall, and put them up safely. And the young man did as the angel commanded him; but they roasted the fish, and ate it. And they (a "good angel" disguised as a young man went with him) both went their way, till they drew near to Ecbatana.

And the young man said to the angel, Brother Azarias, to what use is the heart and the liver and the gall of the fish? And he said unto him, Touching the heart and the liver, if a devil or an evil spirit trouble any, we must make a smoke thereof before the man or the woman, and the party shall be no more vexed. But as for the gall, it is good to anoint a man that hath white films in his eyes, and he shall be healed.

From the book of Tobit, Apocrypha

If I Had My Life

to Live Over

THE BOOK OF GENESIS declares that Adam lived to be a hundred and thirty years, and then, at that tender and inexperienced age, he begat a son in his own likeness. The boy was named Seth.[1] And to Seth, a son of

[1] No relation to the famous Seth Greene: Body green with yellow stripe, hackle red, wings brown and usually woodcock.

Adam's early years,[2] Adam said, "If I had my life to live over again, I would go fishing when I pleased to go fishing, and I would let your mother pick her own apples."

So Adam was the first man who said, "If I had my life to live over again." But after that Seth said the same thing to Enos. And Enos said the same thing to Kenan. And men have been saying it to their sons and daughters, and everyone else, since the beginning, world without end.[3]

If I had my life to live over again, I would fish the high mountain ponds of Maine. I mean those little ponds that are near the top, or at the top, of mountains here in Maine. There are many of them. And if, when I lived my life over again, I lived to be as old as Adam was when he begat Seth, I might be able to boast that I had angled for *Salvelinus* in all the ponds up on the roof of Maine.

I offer this as a suggestion to young men. To my profound regret, I did not realize all that was in store for the man who fished the mountain ponds until the affairs of life, and the entanglements thereof, were as high as the mountains of Maine.

There is a pond near the summit of Coburn Mountain in Somerset County, Maine. I have fished there several times, keeping none of the fish I caught that could be returned to the pond. When one pushed out on a raft from the south end, he could look up on a huge shoulder of the mountain over a foreground of black spruce that bear their small seed cones on spires,

[2] "And all the days that Adam lived were nine hundred and thirty years."
[3] As yet.

where in the deep twilight one expects to hear bells ringing. Up there the sunsets are gigantic. And at the end of long June days those bursts and floods of color are so overpoweringly magnificent that a man feels as though he were attending a pageant for the King of kings. One must go to the hills for beauty like that at the end of day. And from the summit of the mountain that beauty is an utterness no tongue can tell.

The mountain ponds are great springs, where one might suppose the law of gravitation would make such gushings impossible. And a man might guess that in such high, cold waters the nymphs that are important nourishment for trout would be rare, but many of those little ponds are rich with food for trout. As evidence of that, the mountain trout are usually fat, while in a few high ponds the trout grow to outsizes.

But do not guess that I am going to become evangelical on this subject. If it happens that there are always more anglers who choose to fish in the lowland ponds, so much the happier for men whose joy it is to climb up to their fishing. I fear that if the trout hogs adopted this hobby of mountain fishing they would quickly ruin the trout fishing in the little high ponds. Moreover, they would probably despoil the very mountains.

I saw a series of pictures taken from the air over wild lands. Those pictures were made for lumbermen. One could count the spruce trees, pick out the punkin pines, and follow the course of every wood road and stream. The man who showed them to me was a forester, and he was enthusiastic about their usefulness in his work. But I saw that there was a little pond near the top of a mountain in that region. And I asked the angler's inevitable question, "Are there any trout in that pond?" The forester said, "I don't know. We haven't been up there." It is possible that no man ever fished that little pond—no fisherman since the beginning of Maine. Think of it. Are there trout in that little pond in that basin of granite? Some trouter will find out the answer one of these days. I have seen a few of these mountain ponds that seemed to be fertile in nymphs but as lacking in trout as a raindrop on a banana. And I know that the first of the handsome trout in many of the high ponds were carried[4] up there in buckets. And as a rule the trout thus introduced flourished. Some good fellow, unknown to me, carried the trout to Coburn Mountain Pond. Perhaps he was in love with mountain ponds. And if a young fellow were to follow this hobby of fishing mountain ponds, as I suggest he might, he should plan to stock some of them with lowland trout.

Two men carried twenty trout, brook size, to a little pond on the north side of Moxie Mountain. I know their names, but I will not name them here. The trout grew fabulously. One day one of the men who had stocked that little pond[5] talked with a third fellow. They were all neighbors in a way.

Said the third man, "Did you know that there are trout in the little pond over on the west end of Moxie?"

"You don't say!" said the man who had sweat to get the trout up there. "You don't say!"

"There certainly are. I know, because we caught

[4] "Lugged" is the verb for work like that.
[5] Not to be confused with Mountain Dimmick Pond on Moxie Mountain.

nineteen trout up there day before yesterday. They
were good ones too."

"Did you say that you only got nineteen?"

"Yes, sir. *Nineteen.*"

"Then you better go back, quick as you can."

"Why?"

"Because there's one you didn't get."

There are so many of the mountain ponds in
Maine. A man might go visiting them until his knees
buckled, and still there would be ponds on his list that
he had not seen. But what a delightful way to grow
old. If a man couldn't sleep some night, he could call
those ponds to mind, and by the wizardry that every
mortal has he could "picture" each pond; the way it
looked under high sky or low sky, when it was quiet
as a brooding thrush whose nest was on a mountain
set up in ten million acres of green summer, or when
it was wind-swept and the color of cosmic wrath. Or
perhaps he would remember coming to the mountain
in the early morning, where the sun had come first of
all, while the lowlands waited, or when the sun stood
still at high noon, or when the evening sun set bon-
fires and backfires in the sky, and the thrushes sang
high above the thrushes in the lowlands.

And in his mind's eye he would see the trout rising.

THET'S THE STORY

Thet tells the story! Thet's wut we shall git
By tryin' squirtguns on the burnin' Pit.

Lowell, The Biglow Papers, *No. 11*

Help Save

the Duck Hunters

A LADY of culture and talents made a protracted visit to our town's public schools. She crusaded against cruelty to dumb animals. My daughters came home indoctrinated. And I was informed that the lady wanted me to speak before the school, as a sort of auxiliary, upon the subject so evangelically introduced. The daughters displayed a handsome poster. Two mallards, a drake and a susie, flew across the sheet. And the printer had made them as handsome as gray mallards are. At the bottom of the poster were the words ,"Help Save Us From the Hunters."

I said to my little daughters, "How can I talk to you and your schoolmates about helping to save the ducks from the hunters when I am one of the hunters?" And my daughters said, in a mournful little chorus, "We were afraid of that."

The slogan on that poster is of the muddle that misguided sentimentality creates in the minds of good people. Such a gospel creates confusion and brings about a misappropriation of human sympathy that I think is intolerable. We humans need to be truthful when that is possible. The truth is utterly important, because it is the truth. It is not necessary to shoot straight to be a good man and true, but it is important to feel and to think straight.

History seems to indicate that when men achieve some freedom and leisure from the primitive demands upon them they are in extreme peril. When men have leisure to play and to theorize, it is easy to forget about the inexorables. The necessity for human co-operation and of neighborhood is forgotten. In my lifetime there has been time for pink tea parties for people with mink coats and fifty-cent cigars. Although a desperate part of the earth's population of human beings goes to bed hungry, persons who have too much to eat and to throw away cannot be made aware of that brutal fact. And therefore it is a consequence when men and women are caught up in confusion that there follows a tragic misappropriation of energy and good intent. In this social ambiguity it is possible for men and women to think that there is nothing more urgent to do than to save the ducks from the hunters. People with money will employ persons to crusade in their behalf. And they suffer mild agonies because of man's inhumanity to ducks. All the while, so help us God, hundreds of thousands of little children are going blind, going halt of foot or mind, and millions are never comfortably fed and housed. But that is not the end of it.

While well-meaning persons crusade for ducks, we, the peoples of the world, are going down another steep place to world-wide war, although the stench and misery of the last great war have not been removed far from us. It is time to ask old questions again. Why do men work? I mean, why do men *toil?* And why have men, free men, died on our battlefields? Is it to make the earth safe for ducks? Should we do first things first, or must we always wait until the ducks are happy?

I am rewriting[1] this in the month of January, near the end of the month. This has been a cold day. Out on the hill, beyond our town, it was zero weather at high noon. And at twilight it will be twenty below.

[1] This was first published as an editorial in *Field and Stream* years ago, before World War II.

The great hardwoods on the hills will crack in the cold. A pair of Ruffed Grouse will come in on soft wings to bud in a yellow birch tree that was a century old when Benedict Arnold led a little American army through this valley on a venture that ended at the walls of Quebec. I would like to entertain the evangelists for ducks in such a setting. I would keep them out there while the dusk deepened and the cold came on like an invasion. A white moon would climb into the sky, and there would be white stars in the cold sky that is, at such a time, remote and endless and plainly no man's business at all. At that hour the cold turns the heaviest garments thin. It hurts. And one cannot miss the fact that the winter earth is grim.

But no more than a mile or two away the lights of town would come on, and only a few hundred miles away the lights of the largest city on earth would be burning through all the dark and cold. For the moment those lights might stand for much of man's achievement in a universe that is often grim.

Out in the wilderness, even a little way, one is removed from the comfort and the protection of town and city. And for that time the man knows where his old ancestors were born and how they lived and died. The wilderness is no respecter of persons or living things. It will freeze a man in January quicker than it could freeze a duck. In the winter wilderness the little pink gods of sentimentality curl up and die.

That is not to say that we live in a godless universe. Such an absurdity is another sort of asininity that gets hold of persons who live fatly and easily. The grouse buds in the hardwoods. The squirrel sleeps in his den. The deer browse in their yards. But life does not cuddle any living thing in the winter wilderness, which was once man's home. But such realism must be frozen into a man's hide. It must hurt its way into his mind. The struggle of men for men takes on meaning if one learns the lesson next door to the finalities. Co-operation between men and in neighborhood are not mere ideals. They are necessities.

As for the hunter, and the future, he may go like the heath hen and the passenger pigeon. Shotguns like mine may become museum pieces, with cards that read in the new tongue, "Primitive men used these crude weapons to kill ducks." I am also for a better world, and I am moved by all suffering things. I know that there is an ancient hope for a day when the lion shall lie down with the lamb and the duck hunters with the ducks. But the time for such noble attainment is farther away than folk who make posters and conduct crusades to save the ducks from the hunters are willing to admit. And the muddle they help maintain delays the day when, let us dream, the little children and the very old in this world shall have enough to eat and clean, warm places to lay them down.

IN THAT DAWN

Bliss was it in that dawn to be alive,
But to be young was very heaven!

Wordsworth, The Prelude, *Book XI*

A Hell of a Mess

THE FARTHER BACK I go in my fishing memories, the more delightful and precious the events seem to have been. That is described as nostalgic, a homesickness. But it might be true history, because a healthy boy has more ways to enjoy anything, from a green apple to a summer vacation, than any old fellow that ever lived.

I heard folk talk about trout for several years before I caught one. During those years I knew a farmer's son at school in Granville, Massachusetts.[1] His name was Charlie. He was seven or eight years old. So was I. Charlie boasted that he had caught trout and that he knew a pond where trout lived. And he invited me to go trout fishing with him some Saturday. I made the date. As to that, I wonder if it is a sin to pin down these fellows who make grand gestures and magnificent talk.

Bright and early,[2] I got up and equipped me with an alder pole and a lard pail full of sandwiches and doughnuts. Off I went to Charlie's house and to high adventure.

Charlie lived up in Granville Center. There was a large woodpile in the dooryard where Charlie lived. Charlie's father also lived there. He and Charlie were working at the woodpile when I arrived. And Charlie's father looked at me as if he thought that I was the personification of all the shiftlessness in the world. I felt his speech before he made it. "Young man, if you've come up here thinking to get Charlie off fishing, you can start for home, becuz Charlie

[1] See the book *Doc Blakesley, Angler.*
[2] A most excellent combination for the fisher of trout.

ain't leaving this woodpile until the last stick of it is under cover in the shed."

I looked in vain for the last stick, but it was under a mountain of wood. The sun went out of the day. The sweet syrups of anticipation turned sour, and I feign would have spat them out of my mouth. The world had *not* come to a sudden end, but the best project I could think of had come to this sad end. So there I stood, dinner pail in my left hand and the alder pole in my right. And I was a boy to whom a god with whiskers had spoken. Woodpiles had priority.

I tried to reconcile myself to that outcome. And then a prodigious kicking began out in the barn, which was a few rods south of the woodshed. I remember that the boards on the north side of the barn were nailed on up and down, and they bowed out at every kick. The man went off on the run to save his barn. Charlie knew that the phenomenon needed explaining. "It's the old hoss he got in a swap for an old cream separator. And now's our chance."

I asked, "What chance?"

Charlie must have grown up to be a man of action. He ran inside the woodshed and reappeared with a pole like mine and a can of worms. I must not boast as if I had a remarkable memory for details, but that can said *"Grade-A Tomatoes"* on the label. Charlie led off down the road, until we reached that pond of his. It was a small pond. And even so callow an angler as I was might doubt that there were trout in that pond. The water looked muddy, as if cows, or hippopotamuses, had it for their own. Surely it was not a troutish-looking pond. But Charlie loved it, and his love had endowed it with trout.

There was a boat. I remember that boat. It was five or six feet long, twenty inches wide, and nine inches deep. The ends were square, and there was a seat at each end and no room for a seat in the middle. We embarked. Charlie paddled. Water almost ran over. Charlie headed for a flat rock about in the middle of the pond. I suppose God put that rock where he did for Charlie to fish off it. And I guess that the boat was only to get from shore to the rock.

I felt that the day was like a cup running over with good and gay affairs. But there were no trout. However, if one loves a pond enough he can't help trying to love trout into it. Charlie had tried. He said that there were trout all right. They just were too smart to bite. But when I pushed that point, Charlie admitted that those trout never had bit—not yet.

I caught a bullhead. Charlie was not surprised. It was about five inches long. I stretched it and laid it on the rock, where the hot sun wrinkled it. Bluebottle flies came. They walked up and down on the bullhead.

A frog swam out to the rock and put his front feet on it, while he blinked his golden eyes at us. We laid back to study the blue sky with puffs of white in it. I know what the poet meant when he said that to be young was heaven. God pity the man who does not know that. But, alas, it was as if someone could not put up with happiness like that. A small black dog began to bark at us, while dashing back and forth on the shore.

Charlie said, "That's my dog."

I said, "What of it?"

Charlie was a patient fellow, and he explained, "If the dog is here, Pa ain't far behind."

Pa arrived. And he had a stick off the woodpile in his hand.[3] Shaking the stick at us, he shouted, "You boys git ashore as quick as God'll let you git ashore."

Charlie said to me, "Now we're in a mess."

In that moment of panic and command we got into the boat without caution. It lurched away from the flat rock. It filled with water, level full of water. And it sank slowly. That was a strange experience. The boat was like a slow elevator going down. Charlie and I stood at either end, facing each other. Charlie said, "Now we're in a mess," which was what he had said before.

The boat came to rest on the bottom of the pond. And there we stood with the pond water under our chins. I looked at Charlie. Charlie couldn't swim. Charlie looked at me. I couldn't swim. And Charlie said to me, "Now we're in a hell of a mess!"

Winston Churchill's birthday was yesterday. He and our late and often President Roosevelt drove the wild horses for a while. They were brilliant men. But much that goes on these days indicates what sort of horsemen they were. And it is as Charlie said.

[3] For years I was suspicious of a left-handed person.

THOREAU WENT ICE FISHING

Once, in the winter, many years ago, when I had been cutting holes through the ice in order to catch pickerel, as I stepped ashore I tossed my axe back on the ice, but, as if some evil genius had directed it, it slid four or five rods directly into one of the holes, where the water was twenty-five feet deep. Out of curiosity, I lay down on the ice and looked through the hole, until I saw the axe a little on one side, standing on its head, with its helve erect and gently swaying to and fro with the pulse of the pond; and there it might have stood erect and swaying till in the course of time the handle rotted off, if I had not disturbed it. Making another hole directly over it with an ice chisel which I had, and cutting down the longest birch which I could find in the neighborhood with my knife, I made a slip noose, which I attached to its end, and, letting it down carefully, passed it over the knob of the handle, and drew it up by a line along the birch, and so pulled the axe out again.

Thoreau, Walden

Trout Fishing

Through the Ice

WHILE I AM writing this a winter wind is blowing around the house, rattling and rubbing a frozen lilac bush at the window in front of me, and I cannot tell a lie. When any honest man begins to talk about the joys of fishing through the ice, he has mixed a memory of a pleasant day in midwinter with the majority of midwinter days that are nowhere colder than out on an open expanse of frozen lake.

The blunt truth is that ice fishing is too much discomfort and only a modicum of recompense. We remember that some measure of punishment attends many of our outdoor sports. A duckblind in November is no place for a pink tea party. And shooting a buck with a big set of horns, and two hundred and fifty pounds of hamburg, is much easier than dragging him out of the woods. Furthermore, I remember early-spring trouting expeditions to lakes where the ice was floating around in rafts. Once I went to Cold Stream Pond with Elmer and Milford Baker and John Gordon. The four of us sat in a big rowboat and shivered until the boat began to disintegrate. But ice fishing is austere. It is for Eskimos and is Eskimoan, although the ancient Spartans might have liked it. Trials and grievous hurts happen to ice fishermen. Polite and sensitive members of the human race should not go ice fishing. They should stay at home, where it is possible to act and talk like a human being and not like a lost soul fit only for Dante's hell.[1]

When one prepares to ice fish, he selects a spot over

[1] In Dante's hell Satan is frozen in the ice. Apparently all ice fishermen know this classic, for they invariably speak of winter lake water as being colder than hell.

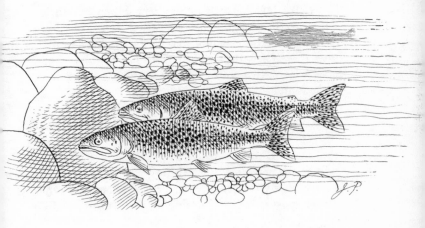

the ice, and there he shovels snow, which is not as deep as it is in the woods, because prevailing winds have blown all the snow off the ice, except three or four feet. When the snow has been shoveled away, the fisherman plants his feet on either side of an imaginary hole and begins to punch an ice chisel up and down, up and down, and so on. Just when the man has accomplished the hole through three or four feet of ice, the water gushes up as cold as forty below zero, the wan February sun slinks off behind a cloud, and the water in the new hole begins to freeze over.

A man may know all that, much more than that, and go back for more of it, but that does not prove it is fun to go ice fishing. It proves that a man's fancy lightly turns to do him harm when he is nice and comfortable and cuddled down in a warm place.

Ice fishing does offer a maximum of exercise and labor for a minimum of pleasure and excitement. There are few hazards or dangers which attend ice fishing, only a few. I once ice fished in a lake where a serpentlike thing had been seen during the summer, but I was safe with four feet of ice between us.[2] But I have known two times when full-grown otters were hooked and hauled up through fishing holes. The otters had swallowed the live bait. Each time the fisherman got away without a scratch.[3] And another thing that makes it easier to ice fish is that one need not worry about his backcasts.

But, nevertheless, ice fishing does entail more deadly bodily exposure and suffering than any other winter sport except swimming. For one thing, getting

[2] I am talking about ice on Maine lakes.
[3] And so did the otters.

wet is part of an ice fisherman's initiation, *Honoris causa*. You see, an "air hole" is a wee place of open water. The habitual, hopeless ice fisherman gets to know where the "air holes" are, or where they are apt to be, but how could the beginner know? So up goes the little red flag on the tipup. The eager fisherman goes the shortest way from where he is to where the red flag waves in the wind. Between lies the "air hole" or the "spring hole." What follows would amuse Edgar Allan Poe. And thus the beginner is initiated by degrees. Each degree is of short duration,[4] being composed of falling into the lake and of getting out of the lake as quickly as possible. Such ordeals are not required of men who follow other ways of angling. If one falls in a river all over while learning to cast a fly, what of it? Such summer brookwater is only pleasantly stimulating. The same holds true of learning to cast a plug or to spin, and all the rest of it. But ice fishing! It is no hurrah to be dropped into twenty feet of natural ice water. Ice may be colder than the water beneath it, but the latent heat in ice water is of small comfort to the man who is submerged in it. Unfrozen water is mighty cold when the top of it is frozen.

But to go on. One must chop a hole to his ice fishing, and then he must wait and wait, but he dare not relax for fear of freezing his feet, or something, or more. Ice fishing is ninety parts waiting. But one dare not take up his traps and go home. He must wait until the dismal February sun sets. And then, just to prove he can endure, he must stay a little longer. A large cheerful fire is the best part of it. And one eats and

[4] If all goes well.

eats. He eats stuff that would give *Pithecanthropus* a pain. And then he says, "I always say that food tastes better outdoors." Ice fishermen say much else than their prayers.

How is ice-fishing coffee made? First, take about so much coffee and dump that into a pail of slowly boiling pond water. Brother, the wind will do the rest. There will be fir sprills in that coffee, and spruce and pine needles, whiskers of lichens off trees, bits of birch bark and moss, all kinds of bark, and wood ashes.[5] It is stout coffee.

And how everlastingly cold one's feet get. One's nose will drip and freeze up. And the fish will not bite. Verily, it seems to me, now, that I will never go ice fishing again. It would be as much fun, and as comfortable, to run up and down Main Street in my nightshirt. But if you do go ice fishing, do not blame me when you get home, if you do get home. I have told the truth, that is, some of it. And I think that the only important truth I have left out is that a man gets fed up with being comfortable and sane.

[5] The list is incomplete. And there is no cover for the tea pail or the coffeepot. Covers are always getting lost.

NO INDEED

Here we feel but the penalty of Adam,
The seasons' difference, as the icey fang
And churlish chiding of the winter's wind,
Which, when it bites and blows upon my body,
Even till I shrink with cold, I smile and say,
"This is no flattery."

As You Like It, *Act II, Scene 1*

Cold-Storage Memories

AFTER WRITING about ice-fishing as I did, my conscience has bothered me. When a man tells the truth, his conscience should support him. But reason and conscience are not always compatible. When reason goes about telling the truth, it must reject some part of the truth to protect the truth from suspicion. For example, if I were to admit that some small part of ice fishing is enjoyable, such as when the trout do bite, then the truth that ice fishing is tortuous is weakened.

I went on two or three expeditions when our vital

food supply was pilfered. Once a pair of red squirrels took our sandwiches and everything but the can of beans. The sandwiches were artfully cached at the tops of several hackmatacks. We got some of it down, but it was hard work. Another time a porcupine with a face as innocent as an anchorite ate everything in our pack, including the hatchet handle and the pack.

What to do in such an emergency came to light when I took my daughters and their chum on an ice-fishing episode. There was plenty of ice on the pond, but no fish bothered our happy tommycods.[1] The daughters, Leah, Jean, and Nellie, and their chum, Shirley, are grown-up young ladies now, and what follows will please them, I am sure.

We were hungry. We were cold and colder. And we were hungrier. Probably Leah and Shirley were brighter than the rest of us, because it was their idea to fry and eat the tommycod that I had purchased for live bait. And they did.

Another time I went ice fishing with my beloved neighbor, Jack Owens. I brought home three trout. They were of a size—that is, they were sixteen inches long. The day had been ten degrees below zero, and those trout had frozen quickly after being dragged out of the river water. The little girls at our house admired the three trout—one for each girl. And they persuaded their mother to put them in a pan of water. The idea was "to see if they would come alive." The pan was an oblong white, enameled affair.

Worldly, but tolerant, I watched that pretty, but naïve, pageant in our kitchen. But the result of the experiment astonished an ice fisherman. Those trout did

[1] Imported live bait.

"come alive." And in that clear water and white pan those trout were a beauty one couldn't forget. But as the water warmed in the kitchen temperature the trout became restless, until the girls could not keep them in the pan. It was a queer experience, and the girls became determined that it was my duty to do one of two things:

1. "Keep them in the bathtub for pets," or

2. "Take them back to the river, so they can be happy."

Maybe this means that if some member of your household should freeze to death while out ice fishing, you might thaw him out in a tub of cold water.

FOR ALL OUTDOORSMEN

Qui me amat, amet et canem meum.
[Who loves me will love my dog also.]
St. Bernard of Clairvaux, Sermo Primus

How to Be

an Outdoorsman

THIS IS ABOUT a friend of mine and how he became an outdoorsman. He owned a small and timid setter. He also owned an egg-eating pointer and a windy fox hound. He boarded the pointer and the fox hound on a farm, where there was room enough and no love lost. This man had a propensity to own worthless dogs. Yet if there ever was a man who deserved to own a good dog, it was this friend of mine—whose name I dare not mention—because his wife is a holy terror, although it is only fair to say that she was not to blame for the dogs that my friend collected.

The little setter was a bitch. She lacked spunk. She was pitifully afraid of everything, including my friend's wife. She had (I mean the setter) every useless quality and quantity that were ever assembled in one setter. And we who were my friend's well-wishers always advised him to get rid of her. (I still mean the setter.)

He used up more patience than Job ever had to teach that bitch what a half-bright setter would have known instinctively. It was sad. And one day when she capped the climax, she had wasted a golden afternoon in October as cheerfully as if such days were not to be cherished.

Perhaps I should have called this report "How To Break a Setter of Hunting Ruffed Grouse, Woodcock, etc.," but I like the title that I wrote down in the first place. And as I started out to say, on that particular afternoon in October my friend had flushed eleven partridges and three woodcock. And all the while the little setter had followed at his heels. The only time she acted interested, and as if she was present, was when a blackberry brier scratched her nose while she was trying to go by it with as little trouble as possible. That was the way the afternoon had gone, and the little setter did not care.

Therefore my friend had arrived at a conclusion. His wife was right. He must get rid of the little setter. And since he was the kindest and most gentle fellow that had ever voted for Harry Truman, he was feeling most tragically situated and involved. *And then it happened*. The time was middle of October 1951. And that year was a prodigious apple year in the upper Kennebec Valley. All the wild apple trees were loaded down with fruit. Not only was there an abundance of apples, but the wild apples were double the normal size. Applely speaking, 1951 was a phenomenal year.

My friend came to a robust tree that was fruited full of a brilliant red apple. Now there are five hundred wild apple trees that bear yellow or green fruit to one that produces a red apple. So my friend paused to taste the wild red fruit. He said that those red apples had a most unusual taste, a pleasant spicy flavor. And it was while our friend was filling a jacket pocket with the red apples that the most amazing event happened.

The little bitch crept up front. That was something, but when she stiffened into a classic point, like a setter in a picture book, that was it! It was surpassing strange and miraculous. For there she stood, quivering from her sensitive nose to the end of her beautiful tail. She stood there in the golden sunlight of the late afternoon, pointing at a bed of brown ferns and red wild raspberry canes. And my friend is just the sentimentalist to be profoundly moved by such a sight. He thought that his setter had come into her own. And there she stood.

He felt that he must be sure to shoot that grouse or, maybe, woodcock. Gun loaded, held lightly, my friend relaxed his shoulder and arm muscles under his hunting coat and walked up on his setter, all the while talking to her comfortingly, reassuringly, and adoringly. She held true and firm to the point. My friend stepped ahead of her, determined to down that par-

tridge when it rose from the ferns, if it was the last
thing he ever did in a world where setters that point
and hold like that are not as common as setters that do
not. But no grouse arose on roaring wings, a brown
bird up out of the brown ferns. And no woodcock
sprang up into the wind on whistling wings, and no
pheasant pheasanted upward. I know what you are
thinking. You are guessing that the little bitch was
pointing at a rabbit. She was not. And now you are
presuming that she was just false-pointing. She was
not.

Of course, my friend was disappointed, but he was a
man who was acquainted with disappointments. So
he made up his mind that he would tramp down every
fern and brier in the patch before he admitted that
his setter was such an idiot as to point pointlessly.
While he tramped about, the little setter continued to
point and to tremble. My friend intended to make
sure, one way or the other. If it proved that she was
so foolish as to put on a show to no purpose, she might
stay on point until the snows drifted about her and
she froze to death as did the greatest setter of them
all.[1]

As for the denouement, it was a sad affair. I do not
know what that small shivering skunk was doing
among the ferns. I only know what he did. And if you
are wondering what all that had to do with becoming
an outdoorsman, I will tell you. It was by design, and
not an accident, I mentioned that my friend was married. Now, after the above, she refused to let the poor

[1] A reference to an apocryphal setter that found a covey of quail
and stayed on point in a blizzard until he froze to death. The legend
does not say what became of the quail.

fellow, her pathetically plastered husband, into his own house. Burke said that a man's house was his castle, but Mr. Burke was sadly mistaken or times have sadly changed this or that. Anyway, there was my friend, bereft, forlorn, and odious. He could not go to a hotel. He would not ask a neighbor to take him in. He might have slept in his garage, but his wife refused him that sanctuary on the grounds that he would debauch the family car. So for nine long nights in a row he slept in his small son's pup tent, after promising to purchase a new tent for the boy. And my friend told me that for the first time in his long and gentle life he realized what it meant to be an outdoorsman.

You are wondering, I hope, what became of the little bitch. It was this way: in the moment of his extreme agitation my friend had shot the skunk.[2] And the little setter had rushed in as if to retrieve.[3] So she slept with the outdoorsman in the pup tent. And since misery loves company, that was the beginning of a long friendship until the little bitch died and went to heaven, where Saint Peter was glad to see her.

[2] But too late.
[3] But didn't.

WILDERNESS AND ADVENTURE

I found in myself, and still find, an instinct toward a higher, or, as it is named, spiritual life, as do most men, and another toward a primitive rank and savage one, and I reverence them both. I love the wild not less than the good. The wildness and adventure that are in fishing still recommend it to me. I like sometimes to take rank hold on life and spend my day more as the animals do. Perhaps I have owed to this employment and to hunting, when quite young, my closest acquaintance with Nature.

Thoreau, Walden

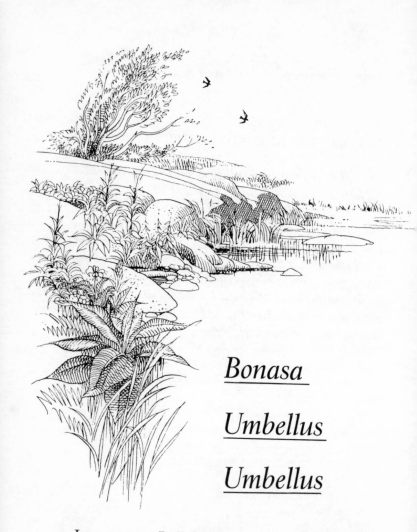

Bonasa

Umbellus

Umbellus

I HAVE BEEN Ruffed Grouse hunting again. I have
been walking about in the tawny, russet-painted
brush and wild growth in a world of quiet, calm, and

beauty. That is, I have lately come home after one more delightful afternoon spent at partridge hunting.

After thinking it over I have concluded, and painfully, that I am a dub, an awkward and unskilled person. I missed the first grouse I shot at. That was more than forty years ago. And I missed the last grouse two hours ago. I am not one of those remarkable persons who only point a shotgun, pull its trigger, and then down goes the grouse, dead as a sofa pillow. I aim my shotgun at the rising bird, pull, and let her go. Eight times out of ten that grouse goes on as high, and as wide, and as handsome as it pleases, which, let me soberly say, is very high, wide, and handsome.

Today is the first of October. While driving down a country road, I saw a grouse rise on his stubby wings. That grouse must have been flying forty miles an hour when three car lengths ahead. I had been idling along, bent on enjoying the moments. I might have "clocked" that grouse, for it flew straight down the road, until it banked and rode off like a glider who was sure of himself and contemptuous of slower things.

And now I must abandon customary usage, because there is no way to spell Grouse but with a capital G. I suppose that one might spell pa'tridge with a small first letter. And I have noticed that persons who usually call Grouse "pa'tridge" call the birds "Ruffled Grouse," when they are putting on airs. It would be brighter to call the hunter of the Ruffed Grouse a ruffled hunter, because he often is. That is, he is often disturbed, discomposed, and even irritated, so cunning and swift is the Grouse of the uplands.

But the hunting for the Ruffed Grouse is the most

delightful of nimrodish endeavors and adventures, because this Grouse is the best and keenest of the several species. And the charm of October in New England uplands is partly the charm of this bird. It isn't possible to predict what this strategist with a ruff will do next. There should be a law of averages to betray *Bonasa so-and-so*[1] once in a while. But he is apt to find an out each time, although the hunter may find him in the same place several times during the hunting season. He went out this way last time, but he goes out the other way next time. There are hunters whose skill with a shotgun is so keen that a Grouse on the wing in front of them, or even behind them when it rises, is quickly reduced to a pa'tridge. But all my hunts for this best of game birds have been affairs of keen intensity, nervous delight, and wistfulness. But my sense of frustration has been a compliment to the drummer or his consort.[2]

I have a story about a Grouse that prevented a sorry suicide. The old man had been a hunter after Grouse all his active days, until he suffered a shock and was only able to go outdoors in a wheelchair. On the good days his daughter pushed him out on the big lawn in front of his house, facing a river and a mountain. There was a day in October. But the leaves, such as were left, were rags and tags of a departed glory. The

[1] The generic name, *Bonasa,* is derived from the Greek *Bovayus* and the Latin *Bonasus,* meaning a bison, or the bison's bellowing. The specific name, *umbellus,* is a Latin word meaning an umbel or umbrella, descriptive of the bird's ruffs. The genus *Bonasa* is the only one found in North America and has but one species. See an excellent book, *The Ruffed Grouse,* by Frank C. Edminster, published in 1947.

[2] For a little while during early springtime.

crippled man, slumped down in the wheelchair, was sorely depressed.

As a whim, so it seemed to his daughter, he had asked to wear his old hunting coat. There were two shells, number sixes, in a pocket. After a while he called, "Mary, my dear, bring my shotgun and cleaning kit. I want to clean and shine the old gun once more." The daughter brought the shotgun. The old man waited until she had gone back to the house. Then he loaded the gun. He intended. He bided his time, thinking painfully of Octobers.

He was aroused from his bitter revery by an old familiar sound, the sound made by those short, stout wings going for all they could, hell-bent for election as it were. The Grouse swept down on the old man in the wheelchair. And when it would have swept on, the old man pulled on it, swinging the gun a little past the bird. The timing by man and bird was right. Down went the Grouse, autumn feathers all awry. The good daughter came running down from the house. Several neighbors followed. The blast of the shotgun was an unusual sound in that quiet neighborhood. The old man broke his gun, removed the unused shell, laughed, and pointed to the dead Grouse.

Grouse stage mad flights. Who knows why? The Grouse do not know why. Even all the experts[3] at shooting Grouse on the wing do not know why. But Grouse do fly into towns once in a while, careening sometimes pell-mell into the side of a house or through windows. And I have been told about a preacher who was eloquently preaching from the text about the birds of the air having their nest and all

[3] And theirs be the honor forever.

that when a Grouse flew in an open window, across the audience, width-wise, and out through the window on the opposite side of the church, which was not open. The preacher couldn't finish his sermon, because half the men in that audience were Grouse hunters, and so was he. But before the benediction, they took up a special collection to pay for the broken window. One old-timer put in a twenty-dollar bill. He said it was worth it.

Lord, so long as I live, keep me alive to the golden hours of October and this delectable land. Amen.

GENTLEMEN OF THE JURY

Plus on apprend à connaître l'homme, plus on apprend à estimer le chien.

[The more one comes to know men, the more one comes to admire the dog.]

Joussenel, *quoted by Paul Franche,*
La Légende Dorée des Bêtes, *p. 191*

About a Hound Dog

THIS NIGHT I have been reading about dogs. I quote: "From long association with man, the dog has become the most intelligent of beasts." I am impressed by that assumptiveness, but I do not believe a word of it. Dogs are the least spoiled of the beasts that have been compelled to live near men.

Once I went to a different hunting than ever a wild pack followed. When we called it off, there were

twenty million men, women, and children rotting in, and out of, graves all over Europe and the Near East. Meanwhile the material treasure we had been so keen about had gone into the devil's caldron where it had boiled down to a stench and a blackness that was bitter and hard to take. At his worst *Homo sapiens* is the unspeakable beast.[1]

A hound dog is a hunter. There are persons who look with sincere distaste and disapproval on hunters and hunting dogs.[2] And I almost understand. But there are individuals whom I do not respect in their queer judgments. I know such a person, who is like a

[1] That has been said in all tongues, at all places, and in all times.
[2] In the order named.

barren place. All normal emotions have been starved. This is a neuter[3] person who stands in a front window, supposing that the Whole is visible from the stance. That person is "civilized."[4] That person's mind has been washed, rinsed, and hung out to dry. Of all the sorts of human minds I have known, that sort of person's mind is the least like a dog's mind. I remember that L. P. Jacks, the English philosopher, once observed that dogs do not live as though life were a spectacle in space but as an experience in time. I suppose that the average dog wouldn't understand that, but the philosopher indicated, as I see it, how wondrously intelligent a dog may be. But I find that I am expressing *my* opinions, which is a mannish custom.

I intend to write about a hound dog. And a writer, like a preacher, should abide with his text. The big book I have been reading states that all dogs belong to the genus *Canis,* although there are distinct *genera.* Some dogs have wolves in their backgrounds, while others had jackal ancestors. And this learned tome considers derivations. The word *dog* is an old noun. It belonged amid primitive vocabulary. There was an ancient Anglo-Saxon word, *docga.* In the beginning my barbarian forebears called him *Docga.* That was when the primal nights were long and dark. There is no black these nights so black as that black was. And then weird, huge beasts called horrifically to each other or screamed in fright or pain. There were nightmares indeed. The man-child who was not afraid in that darkness didn't live to be anyone's father.

[3] But not neutral.
[4] It is well to remember that "civilization" itself is a comparatively new word.

Man began to make his own fires and to feed those watch fires. The fire was a comfort and protection when the night was darkest and most fear-full. All those campfires burned on the other side of history.

The dog came in out of that night to sleep in the man's camp. He came to be man's friend in the beginning, which is an evidence that the first men were better fellows than the anthropologists have supposed. In the dog there was an instinct to stand guard. And the woman's children loved the dog. The man and the dog worked co-operatively. They kept the watch together. They held the creatures of the night at bay, actually, not figuratively or maybe. The man called his first friend *Docga*. It is a quiet word and a good name. The dog answered to his new name.

Now, to go on about this hound that lived at my house. We went out, in times past, where the heavy hand of winter laid hold on one. In a sense we went out to the earthy finalities. My hound was a thoroughbred, but he made no count of that. He lived in my house, and he obeyed the rules. But he thought the outside world was his own. He was always on the trail of the earth-earthy. I mean that literally and not as some moralists use the term. It seemed to me that he was a loudmouthed mystic. And if he did not sum up to a personality, let the guardians of our language find me another word for a dog's being. I shall need it if I may not think of that hound as a personality.

Surely he was never jackal-like. When death came at him, and pain ran through him like hot blades, he only cried for me to stand by. I put my hand on his head, and his eyes thanked me. I knelt over him, and he was content and quiet.

There was always a wilderness in his heart. He paid no heed to a storm. And often, when we went hunting, it was difficult to call him in at night, to bring him back to town. He came, but reluctantly. When he died, I went out into the night, the after-midnight. The air and wind were white with a confusion of new snow.

But I must get back to my text. What was that text? Now I remember. But I must change it and have it read this way, From long association with dogs, man has become a better man.

THAN SUCH A ROMAN

I had rather be a dog, and bay the moon,
Than such a Roman.
                    Julius Caesar, *Act IV*, *Scene 3*, *l.27*

The Porcupine

Is a Roman

WHAT IS THE Latin for porcupine? I do not know.
And I cannot think of another creature for whom a
Latin designation would be so inappropriate. But let
us look it up. It is *Erethizon dorsatum*. For all that,
here comes old Porky down the tote road apparently
haphazardly organized and only halfheartedly inhabited.

He is an independent. And we do not know much
about his ways and means. Now and then some
woodsman who has lived with porcupines writes
something authentic about porcupines, but the dorsa-
tology seems to go to waste. Professional naturalists

do not know much about porcupines. *Erethizon dorsatum* is a quilly reticent. And one may be sure that vacationists, who enclose from two to twenty quills with a postscript—"These are porcupine quills. Our guide declares that these queer animals can throw their quills as much as twenty feet"[1]—cannot be expected to add much to the subject.

Some folks are bright and schooled. Their opinions on many subjects are valuable, but such folks are apt to have mental images of porcupines that do

[1] How happy a porcupine would be if he could throw a quill as far as some guides can throw the bull.

not conform with porcupinology. A porcupine does not sustain admiration, unless a person admires mere protoplasmic solemnity.

A porcupine must have something other than a stomach for the digestion of things eaten, say, a vat lined with indissoluble stuff, or a rig like a beater machine used in a paper mill. A porcupine will eat anything that appears as if it would taste evilly. It would be silly to attempt a list of things that porcupine have eaten. Porky's taste is catholic.

And they are ag'iners. There never would have been a Tower of Babel problem for us men[2] if porcupines had been around, because they would have gnawed it down at the start, the first night, and while they were at it they would have destroyed the wooden handles on all the tools, the wheels, and the blueprints.

Some woodsmen call the porcupine a "hedgehog." But hedgehogs are one thing that did not come over in the *Mayflower*. And woodsmen know that the porcupine is not a hedgehog, but the last three letters in the English compound are so right they retain the whole for the sake of euphony.

One cannot overemphasize the fact that a porcupine is the most exclusive of animals. A grizzly bear is heartily sociable when compared with a porcupine. Of course, the porcupine considers himself a jolly good fellow among his own kind. Indeed, they are vocally and socially enthusiastic among themselves, in spite of the fact that they are dim-witted, dimly motivated, and half-animated creatures. But their armored selves and terribly quilled tails are turned on

[2] See Genesis XI: 1–9.

the rest of the creation. Foxes attack porcupines, but only as an occasional indiscretion. The fisher, or black cat, is Porky's enemy. And old fishers are more or less pinned up with porcupine quills. The underside of a porky is as tender as the cheek of a ripe Bartlett pear. Therefore the predators try to get the porcupine upside down. Lynx also attack porcupine, when they are that hungry.

In spite of his foes, Porky keeps the commandment to be fruitful, and if he were left alone, he would replenish the earth with porcupines. He is a prodigious vegetarian. I heard two neighbors of mine talking. One of them said, "Hear you've been in to your camp." The answer was, "In a way, yes, and in a way, no."

"How's that?"

"Camp was gone. Just some of the tin roofing left."

"Burn down?"

"No. Hedgehogs."

"Oh."

And my late fellow townsman, Charles Malloy, was, I think, our foremost authority on porcupines. He should be, after eighty years as a woodsman, guide, and commentator. Charles asked me one day, "Did you ever hear porcupines talkin' among themselves?" I said that I had. And Charles said, "Sound jist like a bunch of Eyetalians, don't they?"[3]

Porcupine talk is the most interesting thing about a porcupine. The adult porcupine's vocabulary is astonishingly large, and that proves that talking has little to do with degree of intelligence. They talk among themselves with emphasis and emotion. But, as

[3] A porcupine does have a Roman nose.

yet, what they have to say about the exigencies remains a dark mystery to men.

To almost any man who goes into the big woods to stay a while the porcupine is an utter nuisance because of his propensity to eat at anything and everything from ax handles to zithers, but when other animals are holed up and sleeping out the weather, one can usually find Porky up in an old hemlock, nibbling off the last summer's growth, and grumbling everlastingly about the below-zero weather.

FAR FROM THE MADDING
CROWD'S IGNOBLE STRIFE*

*To Mrs. Jacobs, I said, "My dear, we are going as far
as a car can go; and then we walk where God is by
Himself."*

"If It Returns with Scars"

*A trout is purty in any light. I've always said that
thar ain't no other fish like a nice trout. An' they're
firm an' pink-meated inside, givin' the lie to that old
saw that beauty is only skin-deep.*

"And the Sun Stood Still"

* Gray, "Elegy Written in a Country Churchyard"

Where to Fish for Trout
in Maine

IT IS BEST to tell the truth, although one's ego whimpers at the sting of it. Once a prolific and happy writer came to chat with me. He talked. He said, "I presume that you receive a quantity of fan mail." I told him the truth, that 90 per cent of the men and women who have written to me, praising the Dud Dean stories, revealed that they only wanted to lead

me toward their ends. The following note might serve as an example.

DEAR SIR,

After reading your stories for years, I say that you are a great writer and sportsman. I plan to fish in Maine this summer. Please tell me where you catch the big trout and salmon you write about.

Admiringly yours,
OSEPH FONTINELLIE

That was what most of them wanted. They wanted me to tell them where they might catch *big* trout. There never was an angler so far down under the equator that did not want to catch trout. I have known men who only caught cusk,[1] but all the while they wanted to catch trout.

[1] Burbot, ling, lake lawyer, eelpout, mud blower, gudgeon, or *Lota maculosa*.

For a long time I answered those stampless letters and tried to tell each letter writer where there were trout for the catching. I was Maine's busiest, unpaid, unsung, and undone publicity agent. But in the end I gave it up. And for several years I have answered all such letters: "Try Moosehead Lake."

Moosehead is the largest lake in Maine. There was a time when some folks claimed that Moosehead was the largest lake within the boundaries of one state in the United States. If one said that quickly enough, someone might think that Moosehead was the largest lake in the United States.

In old-time Maine the word *lake* meant an inland sea. There are fifty thousand lakes, ponds, and bogs in Maine, but there were only three or four lakes in the old days. Moosehead was a lake. The first Yankee explorer to see Moosehead said, "By gum, thar's a *lake*." I do not know who discovered that Moosehead Lake was not the largest body of fresh water contained in one state, but he was too smart. After that I heard one of our older citizens exclaim, "Who started that lie that they've got a lake down in Florida that is bigger'n Moosehead?"

Much as I dislike the fact, it appears that some of the figures are straight enough. Okeechobee is one thousand, two hundred and fifty square miles of water. But Okeechobee is only about fifteen or eighteen feet deep.[2] Therefore it is only a mud puddle, that is, an almighty big mud puddle.

When we talk about a lake in Maine, we mean something like Moosehead Lake. There are two hun-

[2] Figures are from *Encyclopaedia Britannica,* Fourteenth Edition, Vol. 9, p. 396.

dred and forty-six feet of lake water off Farm Island in Moosehead. Of course, that isn't so deep as some of the old stories about the depth of Moosehead. They were deep. All in all, there are more than seventy-four thousand, eight hundred and ninety acres of trout water in Moosehead Lake. And even when one has allowed for all the shallow water, like parts of Spencer Bay, North Bay, and Lily Bay, there is an average depth of fifty-four feet and six inches. Moosehead is a magnificent body of clean water.

But if pond water froze as deeply in Florida as it does in Maine, Okeechobee would freeze to the bottom. The mud bottom couldn't hold up such a load. Okeechobee would disappear, sink out of sight. It takes deep water to make a pond in Maine. Even if Okeechobee were spread out all over Florida, it would not be a lake. It would be less a lake than it is now and more of a mud puddle.

The water from Moosehead Lake flows down the east branch of the Kennebec. The Kennebec drops a thousand feet or more while flowing one hundred and fifty miles. The Kennebec drains off rapidly. How long would Okeechobee last if it had an outlet like that?

There are two rivers, twenty streams, and untold brooks that feed clean wilderness water into Moosehead Lake. And in the ancient days the Abnakis paddled up the Kennebec or down the inlet streams to Moosehead Lake. The Maine Indians loved that inland sea, when it was calm and blue and patched with the darker blues of cloud and shadow. And they loved it when the lake was black and angry with white-crested waves rolling with the northwest winds.

Kineo Mountain, with its shoulders hunched into the sky and lake, was an Indian treasure house. They made spears and arrowheads of that flint. And Kineo flint is scattered all around Maine. It lies in the graves of the Red Paint men.

Who could ever forget the sight of Kineo, Saddleback, and the Spencers thrust up in the summer sky? And they are austerely noble in the winter scenery. The Indians did not forget. They came to Moosehead to fish for trout and togue,[3] while their artisans, men and women, made good arrowheads and the graygreen spears.

There are as many as twenty-one species of fishes in Moosehead Lake. Some of them are not native to the greatest lake in Maine. The use of live bait for fishing has introduced many worthless fish to our trout lakes of Maine. But in Moosehead there are three of the most prized and sought-for game fish in North America: the brook trout, the togue,[4] and the swift, silver, non-migratory salmon, *Salmo salar sebago*. And there are two species of whitefish, that dainty fish the Indians liked.[5]

I can not think of a nobler place to fish than Moosehead Lake. There is room enough. One will not get stuck in the mud. And if more and more trouters go fishing in Moosehead, there will be, I hope, less and less at trout waters that I love as much.

[3] It is our duty to keep "lake trout" (togue) distinct from *Salvelinus fontinalis*. The "lake trout" is *Gristivomer namaycush,* the browser.
[4] Togue grow up to weigh as much as one hundred pounds in some great waters, but the biggest togue I ever hooked got away.
[5] The Menominee whitefish and the common whitefish, which is *Coregonus clupeiformis*.

ALL THAT MONEY CAN BUY

That man is richest whose pleasures are the cheapest.

Thoreau's Journal

Look Under the Boat

LAST NIGHT I SAW three fishermen sitting on the concrete lake wall in front of a public campsite and picnic
ground at Indian pond.[1] They were full-grown young
men, tall and thickset. And they had powers for con-
centration, at least they were concentrating on fishing
for trout with worms. Last night was a gray night,

[1] Northern Somerset County, Maine.

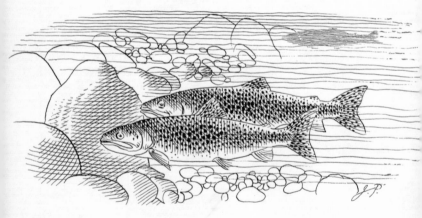

foggy and cloud-bound. There were no sunset colors or bird song to divert a fisherman. And maybe that is excuse enough for the listless, soggy way they sat and fished. Surely their personal existence was at a low ebb.

I should not overlook the contentment there may be in temporary escape from the devil-and-all that lays at a man in this contemporary moment, or, for that matter, perhaps I should consider creaturely goodness that there may be in an escape from the necessity to think. Nevertheless, I have been apprehensive about such a way of living and fishing. So many resources for good are not labeled and in plain sight of a man who lives indifferently.

This summer the royal-purple blossoming of the waterside rhodora is followed, as it passes, by the comeliness of Labrador tea. Neither of these is an overwhelming beauty but will do as examples of the challenging beauty on the margins of trout waters. The wildlands are continually blooming all summer long in pleasing beauty that is perfectly present.

I know that what is one man's meat is another man's poison. But I need time enough to hear, to see, to feel, and to smell. Happier is the fisherman who can use these good senses to enjoy and orient himself on an earth where there are always sources for enjoyment and inspiration.

Years ago we camped with Boy Scouts at Horseshoe Pond in Ten Thousand Acres. Cecil Jewette cooked for us all. The trout fishing in Horseshoe in those days was abundant, and if it isn't someway flippant I would say that it was also glorious. But someone had inspired Cecil with the idea that the trout

fishing in Muddy Pond was more so, and Cecil was
bound to fish in Muddy, which was near Dead Stream
Pond.

I went to keep Cecil company. The day was a hand-
picked day in June.[2] Muddy we found was a small,
shallow pond that would not have been a pond if the
beaver had not built a big dam at the outlet. Elias
Vaughan, who kept Dead Stream Pond Camps, had a
big flat-bottomed boat at Muddy. Probably we made
considerable commotion going up and down little
Muddy in that big boat. And the sun was bright.

What is more disturbing than to be fishing without
the least response or assurance that there are trout
where one fishes? After a while Cecil said, "You
know, I'm thinking someone has been spoofing us.
And I don't think that there's a trout in this damned
place."

I guessed that Cecil was right in both conclusions.
But then I began to consider the shallowness of the
water in Muddy and the clear brightness of the day
and the commotion that we had made poling the boat
about. So I urged that we wait until the sun set and
quiet and confidence were restored.

We let the boat drift. It floated over to the lower,
right-hand side of the pond, where it hung up on
pucker bushes and boggy growths. The water was
about three feet deep.

We had to wait out the afternoon. Cecil was a story-
teller who entertained himself and the other fellow
too. I lolled back and enjoyed Cecil's tales and the
little quiet world, the great blue sky, and the rafts of
white clouds floating along their cumulous, cosmic af-

2 How right Lowell was!

fairs. I heard, I felt, and I looked and smelled. The little pond was encircled by millions of acres of green forest. Its shrubby, boggy margin was gardened with purple rhodora. And it seemed to me that the effect of effortless beauty is unforgettable. Time was, most pleasantly.

But were there any trout?

The objective, to hear, to see, to feel, and to be, prompted me to look under the boat in which we were waiting for the trout to show some sign of being there. The bottom of the boat made a deep shadow. The shadow was alive with nice trout. There was the evidence—not shady evidence, but evidence in the shade. Cecil unfolded.

We waited another hour or so. When the sun set, and wood thrushes began their ventriloquial harmonies, the trout began to rise. As if by summons, they were everywhere all over the pond. And those were brilliantly colored trout, fat, quick, and strenuous.

Cecil said, "And to think that I was on the point of saying we should be going back to camp when you happened to look under the boat."

We should live as big as we can. See, feel, hear, smell, and be sure to look under the boat.

HOW TO MAKE A MAY FLY

First for a May-fly: you may make his body with greenish coloured crewel, or willowish colour, darkening it in most places with waxed silk, or ribbed with black hair; or, some of them, ribbed with silver thread; and such wings, for colour, as you see the fly to have at that season, nay, at that very day, on the water.

Piscator, in The Compleat Angler

The Man I Rowed

ONE DAY, YEARS AGO, I rowed a fisherman around and
around lower Pierce Pond. And that galley work
came about through my own silly sympathy. The
man, I felt, did not belong with those anglers who
had invited him to come with them to Pierce Pond.
He had not intruded. That was not the point, but that

he could not be included. And I was sorry for him, that is, I thought I was sorry for him.

The day I rowed him the utter beauty of a Maine summer encompassed him body and soul, but he was not aware of it. And the fellow could not cast ten feet of line fit to catch a chub. So I suggested that he troll a streamer fly at the end of a long line. That lasted the livelong afternoon, while I rowed him from place to place where men usually caught fish. In all that time he did not talk about anything else than where were the fish and why didn't they bite. He must have had ideas on some other subject, such as taxes or groceries, but he did not reveal them to me. So help me, the great lake was the color of gentians under that glorious sky, but the man I rowed only reiterated, "Where are all them fish them fellers talk about?" I did not know. And in the end I did not care. I had volunteered to row a fellow around Pierce Pond who didn't know how to fish and would never know how to fish for trout.

And then the irony. After a strikeless afternoon and sunset we came down to Gull Rock. I was still rowing after ten miles of rowing and looking at the man whose day was ruined because the fish had not struck as they strike in fishing stories. And at Gull Rock it was past suppertime, as the fellow said more than once. But there were fish rising all around Gull Rock and feeding like pigs on the *Emphemeridae*.

There it was again. And there were two of the fellows who had brought the man I rowed. They were fly fishermen of skill, but they were sick of it. Those salmon and trout had steadfastly refused to touch the dry flies they had offered. There it was again—

that time and place, plus a hatch—but the feeding fish ignored all flies and all fishermen. The two fishermen rowed away, going back to camp. And Charlie Kilhmire's last words were, "You'll be wasting your time." But I had an idea. I had acquired six—just six— fragile but expert imitations of a May fly. Therefore I removed the stout leader from the line belonging to the man I rowed and replaced it with a suitable leader and one of those May flies.

Salmon were literally wallowing around Gull Rock. The man I rowed splashed out that fly as far as ten feet from the boat. It sat there a moment in the dark and gold water, while the hatch went on and big salmon took up the bounty of the hour. Then, abruptly, a large salmon struck my fly on the other fellow's line. The man I rowed pulled up and backward. And the salmon and the fly were gone.

Have you ever tried to teach someone to fly fish when a hatch was on and all the big fish in a big lake were cruising about the boat? I tied on another leader and another fly. Soon after that I tied on the third fly and then the fourth and the fifth. The man I rowed said that my leaders were no good.

When he lost the fifth fly, I picked up my own five-ounce rod, which I had not used that afternoon, and without an explanation I tied the sixth and last fly on my own leader and line. The light was dim. And the hatch was done. I cast several times before a salmon smashed at my fly and hung himself on the hook all in a split second.

The man I rowed wanted to net the salmon. I let him try. The fish was small, a little fellow compared to some that had taken my flies from the man I rowed.

The day was done. Night seemed fluid in the water that laved Gull Rock. What account was the last and smallest salmon?

The light was not good, as the man I rowed said. He tried three times to net that slowly moving fish. And he missed three times. The fourth time he did not miss, because he threw the net down in the boat and grasped the line. And that is how he lost the sixth salmon and my sixth fly.

MAYBE I DON'T LIKE TENTS

I am sure that I should apologize to the tentmakers and all the tent dwellers. Perhaps my dislike of a tent began in a training camp for World War I. We slept in one of those square, middle-pole tents that sleep eight or ten men. A tremendous Florida thunderstorm hit out at the camp, bursting and blasting at the tropical heat. A bolt exploded so near us that we thought the inflated acting-top-sergeant had blown up. When we staggered out into the "company street," we found that the lightning had hit the metal rod in the top of the center pole of the tent in back of our tent. First-aiders were carting away the eight men who had been sheltered in that tent. Some of the eight were still alive.

Tenting in a Tent

New York City, N.Y.
April 1, 1958

DEAR MR. MACDOUGALL,

I am a young man about to be married to a young woman. I am anxious to start right. So I want to fish in Maine and to camp out in God's great out-of-doors. Would you advise me about tents and tenting out?

Yours truly,
WILLIAM MCABOUTOBE

The quickest and most efficient way to learn about how to live in a tent is to join the army. That is the way I learned. Another way is to join the Boy Scouts. However, there are other ways. I once lived in a tent while trapping for fur-bearing animals throughout the month of November. And while fishing for trout in northern Maine, I have camped in tents at various times with Mosquitoes, Black Flies, Midges, and Porcupines.[1]

It is easy to erect a tent. Keep cool. Do not get excited. If your tent is new, there should be printed instructions. If your tent is old and secondhand and there are no blueprints, how about a lean-to? Lean-tos are rustic and professional, whereas tents are plebeian, like an umbrella. You must have noticed that guides always build lean-tos in all the books on how to rough it. In very fact, there are advantages. For an example, you need not carry a lean-to on your back when you move from camp to camp or pay a guide to lug it on his back. And one does not have to buy a lean-to. The materials for its construction are available free of charge where one needs a lean-to. In other words, when one needs a lean-to he cuts down the trees where he needs the lean-to, as Daniel Boone did.

There are, broadly speaking, two kinds of lean-tos. We will call them Number 1 and Number 2.

Number 1. Find two trees that have grown side by side but from six to eight feet apart. Stand between those trees and look straight ahead. Ask yourself, "Is

---

[1] A man I know tells about tenting out with a Rattlesnake in Arizona. However, all the creatures of torment I have mentioned also rate a capital letter.

this a pleasant view? Will I tire of it?" Next, if you
decide the view is all right, take your pack ax and
with it chop down a tree that is only three or four
inches in diameter.[2] This is to be known as the cross
pole. Measure from tree to tree, and add a little to
protrude on either end. That protrusion gives you
something to hang your pack and stuff on[3] or to bump
your head on now and then. Next, measure from the
ground up on each tree about four feet, the minimum,
to eight feet, the maximum, or any height you like.
Mark. Now you are ready to nail, tie, or wire your
crosspole from tree to tree. When that is done, you
have completed the front of your lean-to. The back is
simple. Now chop down twelve fir or spruce trees[4]
about twelve feet high. Bind each tree (meaning the
branches thereof) with wicopy. Do not ask me how
to find wicopy or how to identify it before you find it.
I do not know. But in all the books on how to do this
we are told that the Indians always used wicopy to
bind this or that. And if they could find it, so could
you. Anyhow, when the small spruce are bound, like
Christmas trees ready to be shipped on flat cars or
trucks, place them with their butts on the crosspole up
on front, tips on the ground in back. Doing it that
way, you arrange the trees for a roof, and in such a
way that the rain water will run down and not up. If
you wish, you may cut additional boughs to be laced
into the roof, but it will leak just as much, with or

[2] Don't cut one of the pair of trees just mentioned.
[3] Everything should be hung up around a lean-to, fry pans, foods,
clothes, boots, packs, and game wardens.
[4] Give the twelve trees twenty more years and they would make a
cord of pulp.

without. Now you have a roof over your head, although it will let in everything that it was designed to keep out. I do not know who invented the lean-to, or why. A lean-to made of fir balsam is like a bottle of perfumery. It smells good but is otherwise useless.

Number 2. Of course, you could make a rainproof lean-to with birch bark, yellow or white, but white is best. Any time the sap is running upward, say from May until August, it is not difficult to strip off panels of birch bark for a lean-to. A tree that is large enough to supply such panels is also worth a hundred dollars or more for veneer, but people who live in lean-tos need not worry about the landowners and taxpayers.[5] It is not your fault if the tree dies when its bark is removed. Of course a fox dies when it is skinned, but a birch tree should manage such a crisis with more sense and resource. But none of the writers of books on how to camp, particularly in lean-tos, worry about a few birch trees, although they are worth more than mahogany. Just concentrate on the fact that a birch-bark lean-to is snug. Have a good time and all that.

But I am weary of lean-tos. Let us get back to tents. Tents are ancient and honorable dwellings. Tents were first made of bark or the skins of animals.[6] When people lived in tents, the man of the tent was boss. When people moved from tents to houses, the man of the house was a woman.[7] But let's stick to tents. There are three fundamental types of tents and several modifications thereof. The umbrella tent may be the

[5] They are going to the wall sooner or later. If eventually, why not now?
[6] See an encyclopedia.
[7] Don't mention that to your bride.

easiest to erect. In the old pod auger[8] days it was assumed that an umbrella tent needed a pole at the center. But after ten thousand years of tenting out some nomad in Chicago has discovered that a center pole is superfluous. What does hold up the tent? I don't know. There are six rust-resistant iron rings at the base of the tent. There are also three iron rings at the rear eave. Maybe the rings have something to do with it.

Anyhow, the seams of this tent are lap-felled. Moreover, there is a green plastic screen door to match the forest green of the tent. There are also three green plastic screens, one for a window on each side, and one for a window in back. This plastic netting keeps out all insects and lets in the cool breezes and the rain. But the front awning lowers for storm protection, etc. What more could one want? And the whole thing only weighs about eighty-five pounds— just a handy little pack load.

But there are other tents. Even the catalogue from which I have been quoting admits that. Some of them are not forest green. And some tents require a center pole. Others require a pole for each end. The less desirable of all requires a pole in the middle, three poles in all. And there are ten to twenty stakes which are necessary to hold the thing to terra firma when the wind and the storm conspire to be anti terra firma. But I urge the man who wants to camp far from the inquisitive throng to buy a tent that can be slung over a rope that has been tied from one tree to another. It is easy to set up such a tent, and it is more fun to live in one, because a porcupine or a flying

[8] See ANNU to BALT.

squirrel may chew off one end of the rope, where it is tied to a tree. Then the tent gently settles over one and his dreams; and then he dreams that he is suffocating, drowning, or choking, and when he wakes up, he is.

DINNERTIME IS AT NOON
OR THEREABOUTS

Don't let them mix you up about dinnertime. Our dictionary says of "dinner" that it is a main meal, especially as taken about noon or (now) in the evening. The dictionary is wrong according to Maine usage. What does it mean by "a main meal"? Probably it means the meal when one eats more, or has more to eat, than at other meals. But when a man works hard outdoors, he can eat as much at noon as he can eat at night, or as much at night as he eats at noon, if not as much for breakfast as any other time.

In the Maine woods, or on the river drives, breakfast came before daylight in the morning. Therefore dinner came at half-past eleven, because a man couldn't wait until noon. Supper came after daylight, as darkness did. Maybe there was a fourth meal, if the days were uncommonly long and hard, but that didn't confuse anyone. Dinner came at noon. Supper was at night, just before one went to bed, and breakfast was just after one got up.

One dinners out when his work is too far from camp to get back at dinner hour. But "to supper out" sounds silly. It sounds as if one were lost and couldn't get back to camp in time for supper.

So one dinners out, but he does not supper out. And to dinner out meant to eat out at dinnertime, when half the day, or more, was done, and one had from dinnertime to dark to go until suppertime.

I hope that everyone perceives how important these distinctions of times and meals are.

Dinnering Out

To DINNER OUT is a Maine idiom. It might mean to go to a restaurant or a hotel, but it does not, because that would be "to eat out." While "to dinner out" means "to eat out" of what has been cooked out. It is a statement meaning what it means, no more or less. The Maine Publicity Bureau has copyrighted these words, "to dinner out," but its officials did not invent the words or the idea. Men who had to eat outdoors invented it. Now it belongs to all of us who enjoy dinnering out. And apparently that includes a multitude.

I have heard persons who had employed Maine guides go off into ecstatic praise and admiration for the cooking served up by some of those grand old scamps. And, in a way, that is the background of the suggestion by a literary agent that I write a book of recipes and outdoor cooking. Like any true son of Maine, I am willing to tackle anything respectable if there is any money in it, but I couldn't get on with

that cookbook assignment because, although this country was founded on codfish, fried clams, baked beans,
and everything else our pioneers could get hold on to
eat, no one bothered about recipes. The rivers were
sometimes running over their banks with tons of
fishes from the sea. There were fat and luscious birds
and beasts of untold numbers. There were flocks that
darkened the sun and herds that sounded like thunder
when they ran. Of all that bounty our forebears ate
and et. But no one bothered about recipes. Hardly
anyone knew how to spell *recipe*.

Good cooks make their own recipes. I asked Waym
Collins, who was a most accomplished camp and
woods cook, how he made his perfect pies. Waym was
embarrassed. "Well," he said, "to make a good pie
you need some apples, and it's jist the same with
mince pies—I mean, you need some mincemeat. And
to make a really good cake you need some flour." By
the way, a few days ago Waym was ninety-one years
old. He invited my wife and me to a dinner he had
cooked from A to Z. The occasion was reported in the
newspaper. A hotel owner in Boston called a nephew
of Waym's, and he said, "I have a place, as a special
cook, for your uncle." The nephew phoned to Waym.
Waym said, "You tell the fellow that the army has
spoken for me."

I tried Dave Pooler, who was an old-time guide and
a great hand at dinnering out. When I asked Dave for
some recipes, he said, "I know what you mean, Mak,
but I never used none. Something like salt or pepper is
better in the long run."

A person who hungers after good, old-fashioned
food does not need recipes. He needs a good cook. A

recipe is a poor substitute for a good cook. But when one must be his own dinnering-out cook, he might do something like this.

First, you will need some fry-pan venison, but if one can't get the venison, moose meat will do. If it is venison, it should be from a barren doe that hadn't been that way too long or a yearling, either sex. Such steaks are fit. Tenderloin does all right. Just remember that to cook steak good you need good steak in the first place. All right. Heat an iron fry pan over a small fire of maple sticks. When the pan is smoking hot, add the steaks. Sear on both sides. Add salt, and now and then use some pepper.

Question: Where can I get venison steak?
Answer: Ask a game warden.

Second, now we come to potatoes. Wash them in a brook. Peel them. Quarter them. Slice them. Drain the gravy out of the fry pan; put it on the steaks. Cover the steaks. Put more fat, or butter, in the pan. Place the sliced potatoes in the pan in an orderly manner.

Question: Where do I find potatoes in the woods?
Answer: Up in Aroostook County, where they grow wild.

Third, biscuits. Biskick, bisbake, and biskit mixes are sold. Buy some, if you cannot mix your own flour, cream of tartar, soda, lard, milk, or spring water. When the dough is mixed, knead it gently until it looks and acts like concrete. Your oven does the rest, providing you can make a small hot fire and keep it burning small and hot.

Those reflector ovens can be purchased from L. L. Bean, Freeport, Maine. Mr. Bean did not invent the reflector oven, although he probably thinks that he did. They fold up in a flat package, and Mr. Bean supplies a compact blueprint for assembling them. The idea, in general, is to set the oven so that the heat from your fire flows into it but the smoke blows somewhere else. It is very simple.

> Question: Can I smoke trout in my reflector oven?
> Answer: You can, but we'll not go into that now.

Finally, desserts. Maine guides always serve desserts. In season you may serve strawberries, raspberries, blueberries, huckleberries, or bananas. Or you may try to bake a cake or a pie in the oven—that is, the top part of either or.

> Question: If I can bake biscuits on the bottom, why can't I bake the cake or pie on its bottom?
> Answer: Biscuits bake from the bottom up and not from the top down. But who said that the bottom of your biscuits would be done?

Oh, tea or coffee. No. You may not use tea bags or some of that powdered coffee. Are you trying to make this easy? Suppose you decided to have coffee. Fill the small pail or tin can with spring water or brook water or just water. Set it over the fire. Wait until the water boils. We mean, let her roll. Remove the pail. By the way, did you know that a person can hold a tin pail of boiling water on the flat of his hand without discomfort? I am told that he can. In fact, I have seen it done. But that isn't necessary. And I did not try it. Now, add one tablespoon of ground coffee for each premeditated cup, and then put in two more, one for the pot and the other in case the pot boils over a little. Boil for five minutes. Take it off. Set the pail in cold water long enough to stop the turnover. Never mind what falls into the coffee while it boils. Just boil everything for five minutes.

> Question: I like cream in my coffee. Where can I get cream in the woods?
>
> Answer: Rope a cow moose. Be sure it is a cow moose before you try to rope it. And do not rope any old cow moose that comes along. Choose a gentle specimen.

In closing, I must admit that the easiest way to get a meal like that is to hire a class-A guide who also happens to be a class-A cook. Such a guide or cook can manage a dinnering out that is so good that one remembers it forever. Moreover, those old-time guides are masterly afterdinner speakers and storytellers. But don't ask such a one to rope the cow moose. You will have to do that yourself, because Maine guides are afraid of moose during the milking season. And therefore they are apt to think that canned milk is just as good as cream.

A THING OF BEAUTY

A thing of beauty is a joy forever:
Its loveliness increases; it will never
Pass into nothingness; but still will keep
A bower quiet for us, and a sleep
Full of sweet dreams, and health, and quiet breathing.

Keats, "Endymion"

When the Shadbush Blows

Dear Mr. McDugle,

          I have just read your article about fly fishing. Do you really believe such tripe? And if you're so smart, why don't they have you answering "Outdoor Questions" in *Field and Stream?*

          Huh,

          Just a Subscriber

It is obvious that I did not favorably impress the writer of the above letter. However, he did put his finger on one of my early vanities. I did desire to be the answerer of questions in that famous department, "Outdoor Questions." And for many years I read those questions and answers with pleasure and profit. Many of the questions were of the how-to-do-it sort.

Like this one: "How can I positively identify the footprints of a fox against that of a small dog?"[1] But some of the questioners were seeking knowledge for knowledge's sake. For an example, "Does a fox wag his tail like a dog?" The answer to that one was that an observer had reported that semi-domesticated foxes wag their tails, apparently when pleased.

"Outdoor Questions" wore out several editors or answerers, but they all died with their boots on. Many of the questions were difficult in more ways than one. Take this one, "Will a frog suffocate if its mouth is held open?"[2] One wonders if the questioner wanted to catch the editor with his mouth open. If so, he was disappointed. The brilliant answerers were never caught,[3] although the questions had to do with every creature that creeps, crawls, climbs, digs, flies, runs, swims, and obeys the first commandment.[4]

I often wished that I might try being an answerer. That is, take a turn at being an expert. And I often made up some answers. For an instance consider that question, "Will a frog suffocate if his mouth is held open?" One good question deserves another. And I should have asked, "Why do you *want* to suffocate a frog?"

In July 1952 there was another question that I

---

[1] A small dog would know the answer to that one.
[2] Izaak Walton, when explaining how to fish for pike with frogs for bait, says, "Put your hook into his mouth, which you may easily do from the middle of April till August; and then the frog's mouth grows up, and he continues so for at least six months without eating . . ."
[3] Publicly.
[4] Genesis 1:22.

would have liked to answer. "This spring I observed a lovely flowering tree which the eastern natives called 'Shadbush' and which was in full bloom while the rest of the woods and fields were still brown. How did this interesting name originate and can you tell me anything more about the tree?" That was the question.

There was no error in Seth Briggs' answer. Seth said that the shadbush takes its name from its habit of coming into bloom at about the time the shad run up the tidal rivers to spawn. But if I had been the answerer, I should have said, "It is evident that you are a Westerner or that you live partway out there. My friend from Chicago, the persons whom you heard calling that 'very lovely flowering tree' a shadbush were *not* eastern natives. Let me set you straight on that. The eastern natives, as such, did not call that 'very lovely flowering tree' a shadbush. And they did not call it *Amelanchier*, although that sounds more like their talk. Even Seth Briggs could not tell you what the eastern natives called a shadbush.

"Seth Briggs sounds the sad note in his reply to you. He says, 'Once the short-lived petals have fallen, the shadbush loses its transient beauty and is hardly distinguishable from other trees or shrubs, except for the characteristic light gray bark on sapling specimens.' That is true, all true, but the eastern natives were more transient.

"You mean, of course, the present-day New Englanders. The older New Englanders were true Yankees, without leaning too heavily on the derivation of the word *Yankee*. Anyhow, that is what the eastern natives call the first men from England and Europe.

If a Yankee had his choice of a shadbush in full bloom or a shad full of spawn, the Yankee would take the fish every time.

"You describe the shadbush as a 'very lovely flowering tree.' That suggests you are a woman, perhaps a very young woman from out West. You are right about the flowering shadbush. It is, indeed, lovely. There are no less than six species of the shadbush in Maine. The sweet, red fruit is called a plum up here on the Kennebec River. In fact, the bush or tree is often called a sugar pear or sugar plum. Our old-timers, who deducted the eastern natives, made hammer handles out of shadbush timber. It is close-grained, like the Yankees. It is as tough and strong as the old Yankees who named it the shadbush. When I see it in bloom, or taste the sweet fruit, I think of the words in Samson's riddle: 'Out of the strong came something sweet.'

"In a way, the shadblow is a lovely emblem of the transcience of our beautiful springtime. Shadblow! When the shad ran up the rivers on their eternal business of perpetuating the species, then the shadbush bloomed.[5] And I am of a mind to add this, which I read in an old letter by the Jesuit, Father Sebastian Rasles, who was a missionary at Old Point, Maine,[6] 'At a certain time they[7] repair to a river a short distance off, where during a month the fish ascend the river in so great quantity that one man could fill fifty thousand barrels of them in a day, if he could have sufficient strength for the work. They are a kind of

[5] The Yankees sometimes said "blowed" for bloomed.
[6] It is supposed that this letter was written in 1722.
[7] He means the Abnakis, who were eastern natives.

great herring very agreeable to the taste when they are fresh; they press forward one upon another a foot in thickness, and they[8] dip them out like water. The savages[9] dry them during eight or ten days, and they live upon them during all the time they sow their lands.'

"The aged Jesuit did not say how large his barrels were, but even fifty thousand smallish barrels of shad would add up to a fair mess of fish for one man in one day if he had the strength. Father Rasles[10] saw the run of spawning shad in the Kennebec River and the shadbush in full bloom. Alas. The self-elected successors to the eastern natives have so abused the great and robust rivers of New England and have so dammed those flowing thoroughfares that the mighty salmon, the sturgeon, and the shad have given up their ghosts. But the shadbush still blows along the Kennebec in the springtime. When our long winter is over, when the *hylas* with the crosses on their backs begin to sing, when the gray geese fly in long lines up the river, then the shadbush blows. It is a sign.

"P.S. I left out an important bit of history about the remarkable utility of the shadbush. The Yankees made fishing rods of it."

[8] Eastern natives.
[9] Eastern natives.
[10] Sebastian Rasles came to old Norridgewock during the last years of the seventeenth century, and he stayed there until death removed him in August 1724.

THE THUMP

Canst thou draw out leviathan with an hook? or his tongue with a cord which thou lettest down?

Job *41:1*

The Almighty Thump

IT HAPPENED IN Cherryfield, Maine. Cherryfield is down on the Narraguagus River in Washington County. Ichabod Willey was the first settler in Cherryfield. Ichabod found that the only available women where flowed the Narraguagus were Abnakis. Ichabod picked out the best-looking and hardiest girl and then taught her how to keep a white man's house. She held up her end until the last war whoop. And Ichabod named the place of his abode Cherryfield.

After a while, when I was a boy seven years old, my brother Walter and I journeyed from Boston to Cherryfield on the rails that were far enough, end on end, to reach around the world. We came to Cherry-

field in the black, summer dark. There were several big sawmills on the river at Cherryfield. Because of that, my first experience of Cherryfield was the sweet, pungent smell of pine and spruce boards and timber. Even now, when I smell pine boards drying in the sun, I am back for a moment getting off the train at Cherryfield.

There is another memory, a loud memory. It is a *thump*, an undiminished, almighty thump on the riverside of a woodshed wall. That thump was so loud and mighty that the old man who owned the woodshed came out to investigate. He thought that we boys were throwing big rocks at his woodshed.

What a thump that was to last so long. It began, as it were, at the end of a stout line attached firmly to a pole as stout as a bean pole. Something giantlike had hold of the hunk of angleworms on the big hook. It was an issue, a contest, and a terrific struggle. I laid back with the strength of every muscle in my seven-year-old back and body. We pulled, the thing in the river and I on the bank. It hung back and clung and contorted. But in the end I won with a great exultation.

The thing gave up, let go, and came up out of the Narraguagus like something shot from a bow. It came up and continued in the broad daylight until it went thump on the woodshed. It was the largest eel ever caught in fresh water, so much as I know about such records. Even the old man who owned the woodshed said that he had never seen a larger eel—a statement which I felt to be too cautious, since that eel was plainly the greatest of all eels.

Ichabod Willey wasn't there, of course, but he must have heard the *thump* where he lay sleeping the sleep of the honest and just in our family burying ground on the farm where my grandmother, Martha Willey Guptil, lived when I caught the eel that made the *thump* that time has not silenced, nor diminished.

Ah, Ichabod Willey. Ah, Cherryfield. Ah, Narraguagus River. Ah, valiant days.

THE TWENTY-FIVE-DOLLAR TROUT

Dud Dean chuckled. "Do yer re-member that twenty-five-dollar trout, Dave?"

"All my life I remember that trout. It was the only big trout that I almost catch. Tell your friends, Dud. Or maybe they think in their heads that we are talking like old men in the sunshine."

"If It Returns with Scars"

I Want Him

THE TITLE SHOULD not deceive the reader. This is not
a love story. And these are not the words of a maiden
lady, young or older. There is a mountain in my part
of Maine that was called Moxie before the famous
beverage of that name was invented.[1] The mountains
of Maine usually have lakes at their feet, and there
are several that neighbor with Moxie.[2] And nearly a

[1] Perhaps this mountain was named after one of the Norridgewock
chiefs, whose name was Moxus.
[2] Baker Pond, Heald Ponds, Big Dimmick, Little Dimmick, etc.

thousand feet above these lakes, in a bowl among old Moxie's ledges, there is a wonderful little pond, which is usually called Mountain Dimmick. I have fished in that little pond when a ragged, ugly wind made the place and my avocation unpleasant. But I have fished up there when the day and the evening were of a quality to delight a man so long as he can remember delightful days. And in that pond's deep water swim the kings of speckled trout.

One can see the upper roofs of Moxie from several

points of view near Bingham. And no one who has seen Moxie, when swept by northwest winds and curried by the storms and tempers of winter, could avoid the shuddering conclusion that weather and world contrive to be relentlessly grim up there on Moxie. Nevertheless, a few weeks of summer transform Moxie by a wizardry such as there is no other. And then Moxie and all the hills that keep it company are "fairy mountains."[3] Such is the homeland of the little mountain pond on the east end, where its overflowing water splashes down to Big Dimmick.

Now there lived in New York City a man who happened to be a descendant of King Solomon. He might have been my cousin, your cousin, or any Yankee's cousin, but this is the way it happened. And he came to Maine to fish for trout. And, of all places where he might have gone, his guide took him up to Moxie Mountain Pond.

The last sunlight of the afternoon was touching Moxie's gray granite, and its harsh, rugged lines were softened to match the mood of the nearby night. The guide paddled his man out on those waters that were light and shadow. And the man held in his hands as fine a split-bamboo rod as ever a fisherman dreamed about.

"Now cast over there," said the guide. The fellow snapped out an expensive line and leader tipped with a Montreal and, higher up, a Parm Belle. The little hooks and the leader and line splashed in the shadow "over there."

A hermit thrush poured out his sweetest song. But the man did not heed the thrush and his song. He kept

[3] See that ever delightful story, "Rip van Winkle."

casting, repeating his splashes along the deep shore. The guide scowled. The mountain-pond trout were crafty, well-fed trout. There were not many of them. They were not crowded. And they took no thought of the morrow.

But it happened. Just as the man's flies fell on the water, breaking the black shadow of an old storm-acquainted cedar, a trout leaped out of the dark water and struck the fly he had seen. It was a once-in-a-lifetime trout with red spots like black-ash berries and spots the color of mountain-ash berries. The man was hooked to a fighter. And, as you should know, by all the rules of the game one must "play" such a trout. The fisherman must match his wits and hands with the instinctive maneuverings of the trout. He must give the big trout line to run when he asks for it—at least when he insists on it. But he must not give the trout too much line. And if one belongs to my school of tactics, he must not allow his line to go slack. The trout must be exhausted before he is brought to the net. Even the best of lines and rods may snap with the strain of such a trial. And as the man's wife said, it would be easier to cut the line and let the beast go free.

But the man pulled. He held the rod behind him and pulled. The guide was horrified. He felt like a man who was being stifled, but he managed to shout, "Let him go! Ease up on him! Let him go!"

Then the man from New York City uttered the sentiments of all novitiates.

"Let him go? Vy should I let him go? I want him!"

It was time for a mighty splash, a turning over and over, as if something wound up was out of control. The man's line fell across his feet. The big trout cleared the water by two feet. The Parm Belle hung like a decoration from the trout's mouth. Then he was gone.

As an earnest citizen of Maine said to me about a similar tragedy:

> "The saddest words of tongue or pen
> Are it warn't to have been."

On the other hand, how much does one want him? There are ways. There are the old rules.[4]

[4] And that's the moral for tomorrow. Goodnight. Tight lines.

AND LOST

The years will bring their anodyne,
But I shall never quite forget
The fish that I had counted mine
And lost before they reached the net.

First verse from Colin Ellis,
"The Devout Angler"

The Big One Gets Away

THE BIG TROUT gets away. Persons who do not fish for trout, and do not know anything about fishing for trout, should not yield to the vacuous temptation to make light of the angler's tale of the big one that got away. They should not laugh and indulge in idle levity as if the fact were fiction. They should not exclaim, "Oh yes, the big one *always* gets away." My friend, the big trout usually gets away. Were it not so, there would not be any big ones. Getting away is how a trout gets to be a bigger and bigger trout. For like all important organisms, trout are not born big. And trout grow slowly. If a trout grows at a fair rate, he is about a foot long when he is four or five years old. Even in the richest of environments trout grow slowly from an impatient point of view. Trout live to be eight years old, or maybe, by reason of cunning, they live to be ten years old. A big trout is an old trout.[1] To be a big trout he had to escape all the hazards and perils along the way. That means getting away from this or that, which meant no good for him, became a habit.

The lines and leaders used by modern anglers are of light material, strong enough to hold the average run of trout, but they are put to the test when a big trout is hooked. When a big fellow is hung on light tackle, he is mad weight. And he knows how to use his weight and his power to advantage. And he knows strategies that are bewildering. And he knows how to use the currents, the snags, and the downhill to get away. The angler who hooks a big trout on his light, fair tackle has his hands full. The big one usually gets away because he can.

I read in an old book about Dean Swift,[2] the satirist, that he fished in the river Thames when he was a boy.

[1] The authorities say that the record trout weighed a few ounces more than fourteen pounds.
[2] His name was Jonathan, and he became the dean of St. Patrick's in Dublin.

One day he felt the tug of a mighty fish that finally got away. And the dean said that the sense of exasperation and disappointment remained with him as a memory all his days. He also made a homily of the memory, but never mind that. The big one got away. And if one cannot imagine what that means to a fisherman, he should hold his tongue and refrain from making facetious remarks. I have seen stout men near to tears when a big one got away. And I have heard words that an asbestos saint could not handle when the big one got away.

Do not presume that anglers are more naïve than the run of men and women. They are not. Nevertheless, none of them doubts a fellow's report of the big one that escaped his fate on the angler's hook. We know. We learned. We believe. There is no reason to doubt a man's report of the big one that got away. To borrow a few words from our beloved poet, Robert Frost, we know that the fisherman will be telling about that big one "with a sigh somewhere ages and ages hence."

We know about the proclivities. We know that water magnifies size and exaggerates weight. But, you see, at the last count the big trout that you lost, and the big trout that I lost, is the mystical trout of all trout.[3] He is the big trout that all of us have lost. He is the big fellow for whom we have all fished since boyhood and for whom we shall continue to fish until heaven. Now do not think that I am saying that the big trout is not a real trout. He is a real trout. He is

[3] See the queer and pleasant book, *No Life So Happy*, by Edwin L. Peterson, for some mysticism about the big trout. And read in Leighton Brewer's *Virgin Water* from p. 163 to 170.

all trout. He is a black predator with spots on him that look like hot buckshot.

I know places, like the handsome pool at the foot of Edgely Dam[4] on Austin Stream, where no one has hooked or seen a big trout for many years. And I know a score of little ponds and big lakes that were, and are, famous among anglers for big trout but where no large fish has been caught for a decade. It is intensive fishing, some of it destructive and illegal, that has brought such a sorry state to pass.[5] But the legend of big trout lives on. I never go to Edgely Dam but that I cast a fly, hoping that one of those old-time fellows, long, wide, shining, and beautiful, will slash up out of the amber water of the pool with his great mouth wide open. But I am too near the edge of the melancholy, and I should not follow this consideration of the haunted waters. Big trout are like one-hundred-dollar bills. The supply does not equal the demand.

Of course it is the excessive catching of small trout, in waters where trout formerly grew to fabulous size, that has so reduced the supply of big trout. Take the trout as often as one may, and as long as one may, and the big trout are foreclosed. But shall we praise the old red gods that now and then a trout grows old and big because getting away became a habit? I have seen such trout of late. I know where there were a few last summer. I saw one feeding on drakes in the moonlight, where an old willow tree brushes the

[4] The old driving dam is washed out.
[5] On second thought, the extensive cutting of forests and the destruction of "cover" along a million little brooks in Maine have done harm and ruin to the trout fishing.

water of the Kennebec. I have seen him year after
year when June flows with the river, making a de-
lightfulness of earth, water, and sky. How has this
big trout survived? Big trout are wise trout and they
often get away. More power to them.

NOR TOO MUCH VINEGAR

Gentlemen, let not prejudice prepossess you. I confess my discourse is like to prove suitable to my recreation, calm and quiet; we seldom take the name of God into our mouths, but it is either to praise him, or pray to him; if others use it vainly in the midst of their recreations, so vainly as if they meant to conjure, I must tell you, it is neither our fault nor our custom; we protest against it. But, pray remember, I accuse nobody; for as I would not make a "watery discourse," so I would remember not to put too much vinegar into it; nor would I raise the reputation of my own art by the diminution or ruin of another's. And so much for the prologue to what I mean to say.

Piscator, in The Compleat Angler

But Don't Cuss

As WE HAVE concluded, the big one gets away. But don't cuss, like one of my neighbors who does not possess enough gray matter to make the grade. That is, anything upgrade is too much for him. He is not equipped for the high places. Nevertheless, he did tell

a memorable tale about hooking a five-pound trout on a Warden's Worry from a raft on Lone Jack Pond. And his account of that strenuous, perilous, and heart-breaking misadventure tops anything of the sort that I have heard from mortal lips. He had that big trout within his grasp, and he did grasp it, but in the end it was gone, gone as if the place thereof would know it no more.

"Honest to God," he said, "my head ached for three days."

In a way, this is a test. If you know what he meant, you are a trouter. If you do not know, you are only one of the many who fish now and then because it is the thing to do now and then.

If you are a *trouter*, let's get on with this. I have in mind a fellow angler who is explosively profane. That is, he talks decently most of the time but is ex-

plodable. Even a small spark can set him off, and then his vocabulary would make a modern novelist blush. Understand, I am not going out of my way to protest against cussing. There are rare occasions in life when there is more need of cussing than of praying, as for example, when some rankly human injustice has been done. But I *only* mean when profanity is a prelude to action. Cussing is incongruous when the big one gets away. Should we make a noise, and an ugly noise at that, when the "once in a lifetime moment has come and gone"?

Thirty-two years ago we were fishing up the Heald, near old-time Dimmick Siding. I remember the day, the *feel* of it. I remember the beauty of that sparkling water, full of sunshine or mixed with shadows. Sometimes there was golden water under one's feet; sometimes there was burnt sienna. What prodigious, spendthrift beauty one may meet during a June day, when he is fishing in a little stream going from nowhere down to the sea!

The doctor led the way, and he came to a place where a tiny isle[1] split the flow of the brook. As a trouter would, he fished in the pool at the lower end, where the brook was one again. And there the doctor hooked a bigger trout than one expected to find in the Heald. I remember it all. As a matter of fact, it all happened in a green-gold world, where the sun shone through the alders that made a tent over the little pool. The odds were for the trout. But Doc skidded that trout up on the little mat of sand and pebbles.

[1] This reminds me of the old puzzle about which came first, the egg or the chicken. Did the little island come first, the brook, second, or the brook first and then the island?

The trout hopped. Doc dropped his rod and plunged at the trout, which was off the hook and getting nearer to the water at each hop. Doc tried to set on the trout. He reached under him, but no trout. He lunged about on his hands and knees. He pawed. He had hold of the trout. He lost hold of it. He did everything a man could do but snap at the trout with his teeth. Alas, the trout went free. The trout was gone only the trout knew where.

Doc stood up, straight as a penguin, and he seemed to explode.

I went off up the brook, leaving him alone, while he told the careless world what had happened to him. And on my way away from that dramatization of everything out of control I hooked the same trout or one that looked like it. That time it ran under a hemlock root, with two turns around it.

And I remembered the speech that Uncle Enos W. Boise, of Blandford, Massachusetts, made when I was a boy. Enos was the representative to Boston. And after that he was the senator. But when Enos was an old man, smart persons contrived a tactic that nearly cost Blandford its post office. There was a public hearing for the citizens. During that session voices were raised and tempers shouted at one another. But the Honorable Enos W. Boise said not a word. He just sat. When a man is old and full of honors, "the fever of this life"[2] does not appeal to him.

[2] I notice that I have used that phrase more than once. It is a remembrance from the old classic prayer by John Henry Newman. And since some of us do not hear it often enough to do us any good, I venture to quote its rugged lines:

"O Lord, support us all day long of this troublous life, until the shadows lengthen, and the evening comes, and the busy

At last a Blandford citizen said to the chairman of the hearing, "Mr. Chairman, some of us would like to hear from our distinguished citizen, Enos W. Boise." The old politician got to his feet and glared about him, seeking out with his old eyes the persons who represented the strategy to do away with Blandford's post office. And he said, "Mr. Chairman, fellow voters, and ladies, I do not wish to use profanity in any form, but I will say, damn and cuss the men who started this agitation." And that was all he said. Then he sat down. The applause was like thunder. And there were a few old men that day who remembered Enos in his prime, and they declared that he never made a better speech.

---

world is hushed, and the fever of life is over, and our work is done. Then, of Thy great mercy, grant us a safe lodging and a holy rest, and peace at the last; through Jesus Christ our Lord. Amen."

"DIFFERENCE OF OPINION"

A little boy attended one of my annual Sunday services for anglers, when I told the story of Jacob of the Bunter Pool. When the service was over, he went home to report to his grandfather.

"And, Grandpa," said the boy, "he let the big fish go back in the river."

"Ayah? Well, I keep all the big ones to take home, and I eat all the little ones before I go home."

Jacob of the Bunter Pool

Boston, Mass.,
Box 592,
July 20, 1944

YOUR REVERENCE,

I just read your story about catching a big salmon in the Kennebec River and then letting it go. Goodnite! Of all the damned foolishness that ever got printed that is tops. Why did you go fishing in the first place, if you didn't want to catch a fish? And why did you go to all that trouble of changing flies from morning to night, if you didn't want that fish? Phooey!

Sincerely, your disgusted Reader.

Bingham, Maine,
July 20, 1958

MY DEAR DISGUSTED READER OF BOSTON,

Fourteen years have passed since you wrote the above letter. May I ask you to read again the story of Jacob of the Bunter Pool?

Sincerely yours,
A. R. M.

The Bunter Pool was up the east branch of the Kennebec from the Forks. I have often walked that winding river-drivers' trail and treasured all the way. Best of all, there is that view from the path north of the high ledges. That sight is fit for Saint Peter and Izaak Walton. One sees a half mile of blue flowing river as it comes down widely and rapidly by the mouth of Moxie Stream and that trouty slick over on the west side. And happy was the man who knew that around that bend and out of sight was the Bunter Pool at the end of the long log barrier built to shunt the logs off the gravels below the water from Cold Stream.

There were no witnesses when I hooked that Jacob salmon at the Bunter Pool. And I refuse to strain to make the truth sound true to doubters. That day I went alone up through the little meadows along the East Branch, up the first long hill, then, leaving the wood road, turning right to follow the drivers' trail down the side of that first ridge, up around the first ledge, then along the level way, past the crumpled camp,[1] down and up around Standup Rips, where the water washed the wall of rock thirty feet below the little path, and on until one came to that long hoss-back, and then over that until one came down to the old Driving Shack, when, glory be, a man looked up the river and saw the bunter and the Bunter Pool.

That day the river was at a high pitch. In the upper Kennebec talk there was a "head on." And so circumstances were *not* right and favorable. But when the water was high and cold, the streamer flies and buck-tails were apt to be the most successful. I tried a big Black Ghost streamer. It was with that fly, and at the first cast, that I coaxed a half-hearted swirl and a turnabout on the bottom of the pool. But when it had happened, I straightway began to doubt that I had seen a fish or so large a fish. It was only a gleam of white as long as my arm. It might have been a big non-migratory salmon or it might have been something like a strip of bark off a log.

I continued to cast the Black Ghost streamer. After minutes of that, when no fish responded, I changed to a Gray Ghost streamer, then to a Green Ghost. And so I went through all my streamer flies and bucktails. And all the while there was no response or sign of a fish in that pool. It was not easy to keep the faith that I had seen a fish turn on the bottom when I cast the first time with the first fly.

[1] When Walter was ten, he and I called it the haunted cabin, and we made a game of passing it in the dark, when we returned from a day upriver.

At the end of streamers and bucktails I tried the Black Ghost again. Then I began to go through all my wet flies, which were number eights, for the most part. When the wet flies failed, I began to tie on dry flies. It had been nine o'clock in the forenoon when I began to fish. It was three o'clock when I began to fish with dry patterns.

Of course, I had not fished steadily and continually. There had been worth-while recesses, when I sat down to review times at the Bunter Pool. Once I had hooked, and lost, four big salmon on small dry flies and light leaders. Once I had filled my big willow creel with a few trout that were needed to feed beloved and deserving guests.

And, sometimes, I sat down and *believed* that I had seen a big salmon swirl under the Black Ghost that morning. Or I only looked up and down the river, loving that East Branch as I have for many years. I saw birds. I heard birds. And I forgot to eat the good lunch in my pack basket. So the day passed until about four o'clock in the afternoon. I had come to the tiny dry flies and to the very fly I thought would be the least of them all. It was a Black Gnat. It cast easily on the light leader and oiled line. It settled on the river a few feet above the place.

Then, without seeming to disturb a drop of water, a big salmon shot straight up out of the water and above the fly. And, going down, he struck the little Black Gnat precisely. It was a swift display of power in a masterly creature. Pricked and tricked, the salmon rose again and again, up and up, trying savagely and bravely to be rid of that outrageous thing that threatened to drown him in his own river. And all the while there was no clumsy, bumbling, or indecisive moment. Often he was at the end of my line and the backing, and I felt his full weight, plus the pull of the current.

I knew that the light leader couldn't hold such weight and power. And I followed after, down that shore of football-size rocks, until I came to the little run-around stream that leaked through the head of the bunter. There I had to risk it all, to use all there was of lift and power in my rod and line.

And I had that fish three times at my feet. And if a man had any heart at all, that was a salmon to pump it faster. He was silver and gold in the sunlight. But as often as I reached for the critter's gill slits[2] so often he raced off into the river again. My right arm was aching. I mean that it was aching like rheumatism.

Once more I fought him in from the plunge and push of the current to my feet. I reached quickly, getting hold with my trigger finger through his gills, and I flung him up on the sand between the rocks and the river. And there he lay. He was beaten out. And then I saw that he only had one eye. The missing eye had been gone a long time. The empty socket was so smoothly healed one might suppose there never had been an eye in that place. But he had survived all the perils of the river, the earth, and the sky. And he had grown unbelievably stout. There is no fresh-water fish that can fight like the non-migratory salmon at his best. And that was the best of them all. With one eye he had seen the little Black Gnat floating over

[2] I had left my landing net at the pool, where I had hooked the salmon. In other words, the landing net was up there about six hundred yards.

him, over the curling water. He had hit that moving target.

Something like the river, in mood and will, was dying at my feet. And I was alone. This was my own affair. No man was there to smile at me when I pulled off my hat. No one was there when I talked aloud, when I said to the dying salmon, "Mister, you are the bravest thing I ever saw. There never was a stouter heart. That little hook fell out of your mouth when I threw you up here. You were so near to your freedom."

And there was no one there when I picked him up. He looked like a dead fish, far gone, anyhow. I held him upright in the clear water. And I saw a miracle happen at my feet and at my finger tips. The goodness and the power of the Kennebec, which was the flavor and the life of a million springs up in the hills and under the hills, went into that salmon. It was the vigor of a hundred miles of river feeding into him. Slowly, slowly life came back to him. And he went away from my hands back to the river.

I put my hat on my head. The day was done. And I did not have a fish to show for all my fishing. Jacob was back, up in the Bunter Pool. It was time to go home. So long, Jacob.

EVENING AND MORNING STARS

Besides all the other urgencies, and that fact Henry David Thoreau had in mind when he said it was a man's duty to make the earth say beans instead of grass, there are the resources of faith for the sustaining of the spirit of man.

And the amazing wonder of our tongues is that now and then men have made these resources evident and available. Poetry is the way men have accomplished talk about the illimitable and the timeless. And there is no such utterance that is nobler than a line from the woeful book of Job about the moment "when the morning stars sang together."

That old, old line lives until now to remind us men of the "law and order" in which we have our being. The evening and the morning stars have always sung together.

The Evidence

at Brandy Pond

THE LITTLE PONDS in the wild lands of Maine are intriguing centers of wildlife. In fact, if one wants to find rare and ancient plants and flowers, he should search along the margins of those little wilderness

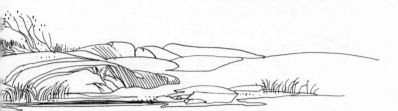

ponds. The long past survives in such places and the little orchids, the white fringed, green fringed, and purple fringed, the rose and whorled pogonias, the twayblades, and the calypso. And there are the many mosses, some of them like flower gardens when looked at with a pocket magnifying glass. Alas, I am not a botanist, and therefore I can't talk about these brevities of the ancient unobtrusive beauty. But I have been a fisherman who tried to look up and down and all around, lest I see less than a *man* might see. And of course the wildlife, all the animals from the tiny to the great, come to these little ponds to feed and drink. One need only wait in the early morning or the after-sunset times to see the animals come down to the little ponds. And as a rule these ponds are rich and fertile pastures for the richly, deeply colored trout, peerless *Salvelinus fontinalis*. Of course, I should not fail to mention that the mosquito and the black fly are also hangers-on.

There is a small pond off the north shore of Rowe Pond up on Pleasant Ridge that is called Brandy Pond. There are many Brandy Ponds. Some of the fishermen who came to Rowe Pond in the old days were hard drinkers. Probably they named Brandy Pond.

I have indicated why I see these tiny ponds as centers of the wilderness beauty, although at first glance they may appear to be unattractive. I can close my eyes and make a picture of little Brandy Pond. It is just big enough to mirror a sunset or an evening star. It is off there, up there in the hills.

No one ever told me that there were big trout in Brandy Pond. But one cold and severe day I left my boat on the shore of Rowe Pond and followed the path over to Brandy Pond. Near the shore of Brandy, and in the trail, was a small circle of ashes and charcoal, where someone had made a fry-pan fire, and lying across the ashes and charcoal was the backbone of a trout. It reached from one side to the other, without a head or tail.

Who caught that trout? Where did he catch it? In Brandy? In Rowe? Whose whimsy was it to stretch the backbone and ribs across the cold ashes of his fire? I do not know.

But I do know one thing, yes, two things, about him, because he gave them away. He was a woodsman at heart. And he practiced what his heart believed. He poured water over his little fire when he had eaten. The charcoal proved that. And he had a pleased and pleasant sense of humor. Stretching the backbone over the dead coals, he gave himself away. He said to his own good company, "If some fisherman comes over this trail before this fragile memento perishes, he will speculate on who caught this trout, who ate it, and where it came from."

Sometimes when I think of Brandy Pond, a little pond in a huge country of trees, I see the black ashes and charcoal and that long trout's backbone stretched from rim to rim. And I can see the clouds of sunset pictured when the wind of the day has died away. And I can see the pale reflection of the evening star. If a pond grows trout, it is a pond to remember. And even the smallest of ponds is significant if it is a trout pond. And there never was a trout pond so small that it didn't reflect the evening and the morning stars.

FOR, LO, THE WINTER IS PAST

For, lo, the winter is past, the rain is over and gone; the flowers appear on the earth; the time of the singing of birds is come, and the voice of the turtle (dove) is heard in our land.

Song of Solomon, 2:11, 12, King James Version

Fried Trout

and Salt Pork

"FOR, LO, the winter is past," and the time for a fry of trout has come. My beloved friend, Dud Dean, says that if ever the time comes when there are no trout available, it will not be spring, whatever the *Farmers' Almanac* says. Spring is the time for a fry of trout. I remember a day, long years ago, when the ice had gone out[1] of Morse Pond. Bob Moore and I walked out by the way of the old Gore Orchard. And when we crossed the ridge beyond the first Morse Pond, where there are no trout, a big white birch lay across the trail. I cut a chip out of the top side of that tree, and when the sap welled into the scarf, we drank the wintergreen-flavored blood of the birch with pleasure. It was a drink of spring.

But fried trout are as good as any flavor that comes with springtime. And a fry of trout is the only reason I have left in me for going fishing before the comforts of June.

Let this be honest. I do not hanker for trout all summer long, but blessed is the trouter who has an appetite and relish for trout when the earth comes alive again after long winter. Then trout are good food, and they are worth all that they cost, which is from ten to twenty dollars a pound, if one charges up

[1] We say, "The ice is going out." That is flat-footed prose that contrives to hide all the lilt and the lift that we feel. Ice going out is a mystical event. It occurs without a tumult of noise. The field of ice over the pond or lake melts, leaving countless spikes or rods of ice. Then when a spring wind moves the mass the wands of ice ring sweetly. Thus it might be said, by those who have heard the sound, that the ice goes out to fairy music. But trust a Yankee to keep that, and the uplift that he feels at this great sign of winter's end, a secret. So he says, meaning all the meaning, "The ice is going out."

the overhead. Thirty-five springtimes ago Dr. Perci-
val Hopkins and I went fishing on Heald Stream,
three miles from Dead Water on the old Somerset
Line. The doctor knew the location of a small pond[2]
on a smaller brook that dribbles into the Heald.[3] That
little pond lay in the burned land north of the main
stream. I am writing this years after. The burned
land is coming up to forest trees again. And Dr. Hopkins went off and away long years ago.[4]

The cold water in that little pond was swarming
with small brook trout. And in Maine there is a tradi-
tion that small trout are the sweetest trout. How
small they should be is a controversy that the Department of Inland Fisheries has not settled yet. On the
left bank, which was about three hundred feet long,
there was a fringe of living cedars that had escaped
the fire, and those cedars were backed by spruce and
fir. The slim spires of the new black growth were
handsome in that pale blue sky. And the hardwoods
were blossoming in various yellows, greens, and reds.

Trout were everywhere in that little pond, everywhere in that golden water. They were all small
trout, six to ten inches long, and they were green and
silver and pink, lacking the vivid colors of summer,
when the water would be darker. The law book said
that one might catch twenty-five of those trout. And
he could! I caught my trout on those old-fashioned
wet flies, whose names are pleasant: Silver Doctor,

---

[2] It was half pond and half beaver flowage.
[3] They pronounce it Hale, like hail.
[4] To my dismay I did not get this book together until Mae Hopkins,
who would have loved this little tale for the doctor's sake, had left
us, although she outlived her husband by several years.

Parm Belle, Montreals, Brown Hackle, Professor, Pink Lady, and Royal Coachman. The trout cared little more for one than the other. The trout were hungry. It was spring again.

The doctor made what he called a "fry-pan fire," where the little brook that fed the pond tumbled in over big granite boulders. When it comes to frying trout, one can fry them in an aluminum mess kit, or an old lard pail, maybe, but there is only one right way to fry trout, and it is to fry 'em in an old-fashioned heavy iron fry pan. There are steel frying pans, and there are aluminum frying pans, with wooden handles that catch on fire, but if a frying pan were made of gold, a woods cook would throw it away, because the difference between a fry pan and a frying pan is that the latter ain't fit.

So we cleaned our trout, all of them. Then when the fry pan began to be hot, Doc laid in strips of fat salt pork. When the pork was done to a light brown, Doc forked it out on a tin plate covered with brown paper. Then he put the trout in side by side. I watched them sizzle, but Doc ignored them while he set up his tea pail and prepared to toast bread. I asked Doc if it were true that salt pork, or much of it, was dangerous to one's physical being. "Let me tell you something," replied Doc, "and don't you ever forget it. When salt pork hurts someone, that person is so far gone it doesn't matter what *she* eats."

We had not eaten since five o'clock in the morning. Therefore we did not need to tell God how grateful we were for the food at noon. God knew. And I do believe that nothing tastes so good as brook trout that have been placed in the fry pan before the brook water dried off them. But one needs a genuine fry pan, plenty of salt pork, and a springtime appetite.

When one has eaten all he can in such a place and day, he settles back on his elbows. The wood smoke from the little fire is sweet. The high sun is friendly warm. And then one wishes he might always go trout fishing as often as he hankered for a fry of trout. Trout are good for what ails a man after the winter, when one has lived on store bread and too much of "the fever of this life," including the income tax. But I must remember, as the old lunkhead said about the rabbit, that first one must catch the trout. For, mind you, the trout must be wild trout. Those hatchery-fostered, liver-fed, vitamin-nourished trout will not do. Even a frying pan is good enough for such trout. But you, my friend, deserve some wild trout and a chance to fry them under the wide heavens when spring is moving in to possess the land.

CONCLUSION

And I am the willinger to justify the pleasant part of it, because, though it is known I can be serious at seasonable times, yet the whole discourse is, or rather was, a picture of my own disposition, especially in such days and times as I have laid aside business, and gone a-fishing with honest Nat. and R. Roe; but they are gone, and with them most of my pleasant hours, even as a shadow that passeth away and returns not.

Introduction, p. xxviii, The Compleat Angler

Tight Lines

AND NOW, brothers of the angle, we have come to the end of this little book, and what shall we say for the good of the ancient fraternity of free hearts and fishers of trout? As I see it, I should feel utterly useless, and personally bereft, if I had nothing else to say, to offer, than a how to hook and kill more trout, a mere wisdom of the craft concerning the fishing for fishes.

Thank God, I have been here on the Kennebec River for many years. During those years, when I was writing the Dud Dean stories and many articles about angling for a trout, or gunning for game, many fishermen came to this parsonage door without fanfare or pretense. They came from near at hand and from miles and miles away, even seas away. They were tall men and short. They were fat men and thin. They were dark or fair, of one race or another. They earned their bread in various professions and vocations. Some were humble so much as this world's fame is concerned. A few of them were famous men. *They were all fishers for trout.*

Every last one of them was a significant person and an important citizen, except a few who must have known that they did not belong in such company.

I have grown too old, and I think too wise, to attempt to draw a line between such men. One of them came to my town in an inebriated state. And without bothering to inquire where I lived, he stumbled out of his car in the center of the business section, straightened up, and began to shout, "Mak, oh, Mak. Where are you, Mak?"

That might have gone on until trouble, but a smart waitress in a restaurant went out and asked, "Are you looking for Mr. Macdougall?" He was. And that is one way to find a man. He came to our famous Anglers' Sunday service the following day, and he was sober as a deacon. And that was the man who put a sound and good check for two thousand dollars in the collection plate. And that was the day we had twenty-three hundred dollars in the collection. I warn all readers that I am not making too much or too little of that. I retell the tale only to emphasize what an astonishing fraternity this is—the fraternity of fishers for trout. Never mind my tears because so many of these excellent gentlemen, and dear souls, are off and away.

There remains to say, briefly and honestly, that it is my conviction and faith that fishing for trout detaches a man from the superficialities that, alas, occupy too many of us, too much and fatefully. And when I cast back, thinking on these many anglers who called at my house "to pass the time of day," and when I try to put my finger on the quality of manhood that was in them, for all the idiosyncrasies and even follies of the flesh, I conclude it was derived from that old-fashioned realization of the earth and sky, land and sea, wind and quiet, sun and rain, and season by season. Please notice that with these men in mind I have not once used the adjectives "noble" or "great," although I do not doubt that some of them were. Plain words alone convey the meaning of the earth, of day and night, of living, of dying, and of immortality.

Tight lines!